I0435011

The Foster Care Dilemma

2nd Edition

By
Johan Wassenaar

26,959 words

January 1, 2015
Authored by: Johan Wassenaar

Contents

Foreword

This literary exposé was designed to familiarize the widest possible audience with the good and the bad of contemporary foster care systems, which far too often diminish and punish the very children they are charged with caring for. In many jurisdictions foster care has become corrupted to yield illegal profits to the facility operators at great expense and suffering to the children in their care.

Most disconcerting is the almost wicked determination of some foster care providers to wreak mindless cruelty on the defenseless children in their care. My expectation was that interviews of children out of foster care would be discomforting, but not to the heartbreaking extent I experienced.

On average, foster care costs the taxpayers as much per child per year as high level private schools charge for educational excellence, while the vast majority of children leaving foster care are almost certain to fail in private life.

Society has no business putting down its most defenseless members in this way and we need to examine our hearts and minds to resist and eradicate the greatest evils in a system that has become hopelessly bureaucratized, inefficient and needlessly expensive. We must be able to look forward to the day when politicians in large jurisdictions are elected partly on how well foster children do in their jurisdiction.

On the bright side, there are State foster care systems that work well by trying to match children in need of care with family members willing to adopt them, rather than to immediately place them in foster homes...while at the same time working diligently with foster parents to do well with their foster children. There are also countless foster parents who take excellent care of their foster children, but they are in the minority in large metropolitan settings where chronic shortages of foster and group homes abound.

Parental drug and alcohol abuse underlies the reason for such large numbers of children needing foster care. Unfortunately, too many children out of foster care wind up becoming addicts themselves and frequently wind up in prison.

It is our intention to follow this exposé with sequential editions to bring increasing depth and insight into its mission by adding the experiences of additional foster care people to keep the message vibrant and more embracing. We hope that this will perpetually refresh and remind the public what foster care should be and to work together to make it happen!

We openly solicit the financial and in-kind participation of those who seek ways of bringing progressive improvements to foster care standards.

To that end, and to raise enough capital to ensure very wide distribution of the publication, we are incorporating "The Foster Care Dilemma" as a California non-profit company and are qualifying it as a 501 (C) (3) Tax Exempt Organization.

We intend to issue a newsletter to promote ideas for additional chapters to include in successive editions of the book. We need your help to create a groundswell of compelling reasons to end the uncalled for violence being directed at defenseless children.

Please contact us at: thefostercaredilemma@gmail.com

Chapter 1, Dan's Childhood

Dan was born in 1993 before it happened, but he always fancied that it meant something special that he was born on 9/11!

His recollections of living in the very rough ghetto on the Near North side of Chicago with his mother and her Puerto Rican companion remain vague. What sticks in his mind is that it was dangerous. He can still see the image of a man walking down a street and being shot repeatedly from a passing car. They left behind what looked like a person bleeding to death, and no one went to help him.

Years later he heard that even the Chicago police refused to go into this hell hole, right in the midst of some of the most opulent luxury developments on the north side of the city, to investigate the many murders being committed there. Gang-violence and neglect created terrible living conditions. He later learned that his mother's companion, presumably his dad, was part of a gang who called themselves the "Latin Kings".

The slum was disintegrating and had lost all sense of organization. Rents were low because few businesses actually came into the area of dilapidated dwellings and the property owners, waiting to sell their land for commercial purposes, allowed it to deteriorate, asking just enough in rent to carry the taxes. Over large stretches of the slum, men neither knew nor trusted their neighbors and a large part of the native population were transient prostitutes, criminals, outlaws and hobos.

He vividly recalls being hauled around the streets by his mother to call on what she termed uncle this or uncle that, who he later discovered were men who hired her to have sex with them. The fact that she was a hooker, made his grandparents want to keep him away from her and from her meager lifestyle.

One of his dad's brothers, who lived in a nice part of Chicago, took him to church to get him away from his mother. His uncle had a good job at a chewing gum factory, had several kids of his own and he loved staying with them. His dad had six other brothers and two sisters as well, so his sister and he were not entirely lacking for family members besides their drug and alcohol addicted mother.

His grandma had dated the same man for some twenty years and he considered his mom to be his daughter. He had five brothers and three sisters who they also visited from time to time.

To get to them they had to go by train or bus. The brown line was closest to their ghetto and its trains fascinated young Dan because some of them ran on the surface next to the highway and then went underground closer in to the city center. Others stayed above ground on elevated tracks above the streets. Those were the older ones. Compared with where they lived, the immediately adjacent part of Chicago felt like a dynamo of wealth and activity.

His mom was very possessive about him and his sister, who was a year older than him. Their best times with his mom were when her bosom friend, who was a night club dancer, came to visit them. His mom stayed sober on those occasions and the dancer paid lots of attention to them, bringing them cute little gifts. As he recalls she was the only real friend his mother had.

There were other moments when his mom wasn't on drugs and they all loved each other. But most of the time she was loaded and unresponsive, so his sister and he clung to each other.

As he later learned, she was forced to hand her welfare stipends over to his dad. He didn't know how and what he contributed, but there was almost no money left to spend on him and his sister. On the rare occasions when his father was home, he tried to be nice to Dan, who didn't trust him because of the way in which he lost his temper and beat him.

His mother had other lovers. One of them was black and it ended in his mother giving birth to his little brown sister.

* * *

By the time he turned seven, there were warrants out for his dad's arrest in Illinois, and he remembered leaving on a Greyhound bus for the long journey to Miami, where other relatives of his mother lived. Along the way, his mother vanished for several days, but then caught up with them again.

It felt good to be in the country away from the Chicago slums. His dad wasn't wanted in Florida which may be why they had moved there.

Once they were settled, the routine wasn't much different than what it had been in Chicago, except that his dad could spend more time with him and took Dan for walks.

On one occasion his dad must have sensed that they were being followed, because he took Dan quickly into a line of tourists boarding a bus headed to a park in the Everglades. Once they were inside the gates of the park, his dad seemed more relaxed and led him down a foot path winding through the dense undergrowth. There were warning signs not to leave the trail because the swamp areas weren't safe. The park was full of wild animals which were illustrated on bill boards every so often. They showed scenes of alligators, vipers and snakes. His dad began to realize that they were being tracked by two Dade County officers.

They came to a spot along the trail where there were benches overlooking a larger open area where there were alligators on the shore line just resting in the sun. Dan was standing next to his dad watching with his heart thumping as they saw the two cops approaching. The step down from the trail was large enough for his dad to hide away and he took Dan with him. While none of the alligators responded to their presence one suddenly rose up onto its feet and stood there with its mouth wide open. His dad turned as pale as a ghost, and was distracted until the cops were upon them. They scared the animal away and had cuffs on his dad before he could recover enough to try running away.

Looking at Dan, he heard one of the cops say: "Young man, you have no idea how fast these critters can move for short distances. You were lucky you didn't get hurt."

"As for you, sir, we think you are wanted by the Chicago police and we will take you to the station for identification and processing."

Dan never forgot the ride in the police cruiser. His dad seemed humbled enough for him to feel sorry for this gangster who caused his mother to keep them in poverty.

Soon after, his dad was extradited, sent back to Chicago, the black man his mother had stopped to be with, joined their family.

Life in Miami was a lot different than in Chicago. The area they lived in was full of Cubans and Dan couldn't speak enough Spanish to understand or answer them. He was given a chance to attend a nursery school, but they only spoke Cuban Spanish. His mother protested and he was finally moved to an English class and that part he really enjoyed. The teacher liked him, because Dan was eager to learn and it took his mind off their poor living conditions.

In spite of all this, his mom still sort of raised him in her drug-filled world and by the time Dan was seven, he at least knew right from wrong. Then something happened with the family in Chicago and they had to move to California where another relative lived.

* * *

There followed another long bus ride, this time to Oildale, a poor township next door to Bakersfield. The only difference was that the men coming to see his mother now were from the oilfield.

If anything, life for the three kids got worse. His sister and Dan had to make do with feeling some kind of love for their mother when she was sober, and that became less often because by then she was shooting up with heroin which left less money for their food and needs.

Dan had many friends in elementary school in Oildale. He was good at sports and loved the school.

Then as his parents became more addicted to drugs, he was forced to move to the poorer 34th Street Community School and lost contact with all his friends. He was ten years old and had to make new friends. He was always really smart in school and the boys responded by trying to bully him, but the girls backed him up.

By the time he was twelve he started to notice the girls more, but he had a terrible case of acne. Then his sister invited her really hot cheer-leader friend over and she liked Dan and turned him on. She got him to smoke cigarettes and weed and to drink booze. Soon they became best friends but she was very sexual and it broke his heart to see her having sex with other boys who came round.

While he was getting to be a cool kid, his sister started smoking, and since their parents showed no interest in them, they began using their place as their party house in which to smoke pot, drink booze and have sex.

He was being acknowledged at his new school and people started approaching him until he had a clique of friends who did nothing but steal stuff, party and chill out with girls.

Some of them tried to bully Dan. At first he was afraid to fight. Then he began fighting back and after he had beaten several of them, his name was known by everyone and he began getting into trouble. He could hustle up things and money better than any of his friends, so he had new clothes, a bike and money in his wallet.

* * *

It was obvious to him that he and his siblings each had different fathers. His older sister by a year was the daughter of a white boyfriend, he was supposed to be the Puerto Rican gangster's son and they knew the black man who was his little sister's father. His "dad" was finally released from jail in Illinois and rejoined them and his mother.

His older sister had her father's parents and family to support her. And his little sister had her grand-parents to help her. That left Dan to hustle on his own.

Over time he became more daring. Young girls liked him and the ones that came on to him would pay him to line them up with dates to get laid. They shared equally in what they were paid.

Dan sometimes peddled cheap drugs like crack cocaine which in Bakersfield they called "rock" cocaine. He sold pellet-size "rocks" in tiny plastic vials for ten bucks a throw. Because of what drugs had done to his mother, he only did this when he was really hard up for cash.

As ever, the one thing he really liked was school, because it was interesting and the teachers treated him with respect.

Chapter 2, Foster Care

By 2007, Dan's family was skating on thin ice and by the time he was 14, still in Oildale, they were without a roof over their heads. The welfare folks took the three kids into custody and Dan got his first taste of life in foster care when he and his siblings were taken into Child Custody Services at the Jamison Center. The staff was responsible for establishing and enforcing support orders when children received public assistance. His older sister went into the custody of her grandmother as did his younger sister who went into the custody of her grandmother. Child Custody is supposed to act in the 'public interest' and not to represent anyone.

They opened Dan's case and since there were no capable parents to turn him over to, he was handed to a children's bureau that handled foster care and adoptions. Their program was to help find safe homes for foster children, from newborn babies to children of 18. They also gave support to foster and adoption parents with resources to accommodate the children.

* * *

Dan was herded into temporary housing in Jamison Center with a great many children coming and going which made it easy for him to simply walk away for several months. He kept going to school, partying with his friends and staying with them or living on the street.

Then the cops charged Dan with stealing a mountain bike and some clothes from a mall and put him on probation. Before he could be sentenced they found out that he came from Child Custody, who refused to take him back, because he had been absent without leave for so long. Probation took custody of Dan and left him in Juvenile Hall where he was kept walking in a locked room with his hands cuffed behind his back.

* * *

Since he got into Juvenile Hall for committing a crime as a foster youth, they put him on foster youth probation, causing him to be a ward of the state and he had his first taste of being held prisoner.

To resolve the issue they finally placed Dan in a group home about a hundred miles to the north in Fresno, which he had to share with four black kids. A group home is supposed to be a place where people wishing to adopt kids go to find them...like people do with dogs at a pound. Dan was there from the beginning of December 2008, until near the end of October 2009.

The cruelest aspect in this group house was that the other four boys were dangerous kids. They ganged up on him for being a "Southerner" while they regarded themselves as "Northerners". They beat him in many ways, and got away with it because most of the staff members were also black and viewed Dan as an outsider.

They jumped him one day and beat him so badly that the staff had to take him to the emergency ward for treatment of his left eye which was swollen shut and his left shoulder that had been dislocated and bruised. After that Dan began to fight back and he soon got to where they respected him.

When they were not in school, they kept them in the house around the clock, and hardly fed or clothed them. They treated them like throw away rubbish considering that they were being paid something like $2,000 a month per foster child.

If you 'left' the home you were in trouble. By that was meant that you had to be in sight of the staff at all times.

Dan found himself being singled out because he didn't take their criticism lying down, like all the others did.

Dan had a room with all the stuff the state required group home owners to provide, but in their home the doors had to stay open all the time and they could and did room searches at any time. One also couldn't go into one's room until it was bedtime. They had to ask to use the bathroom, to eat, or do anything else.

At school, the kids could tell that they were from a group home and all the staff knew too. They had a dress code by group home and they did their own laundry. There were washing machines in the house, but they could only use them on certain wash days.

At most group homes, on holidays, the kids would get a decent meal and maybe some clothes. They were dishing out what they considered suitable clothes. Being from Bakersfield, Dan's taste in clothes was too racy for them. Down south boys preferred baggy pants with split cuffs and knit beanies or baseball caps turned at an angle. Up there they dressed in conventional clothes.

They had to stay indoors, but could play team sports as soon as they got home from school, but it depended on what level one was in the group house.

When you got there you were usually assigned to level one. The better you did, your rank went up towards a top level of five, but it took months to increase upward by a level and if you got into trouble, you could go down in rank. They documented your behavior daily. If you continued to be bad you could get terminated from the program, and eventually end up back in Juvenile Hall.

They had to sign off on different behaviors like cleanliness, attitude, eating and so forth every day.

Dan's only relief was school, where, by law, they had to deliver and fetch them. Dan's problem was that he suffered from an attention-deficit, hyperactivity disorder, so he had to take pills in order to learn and concentrate. That slowed his intake of knowledge, which frustrated him. On top of that, being strictly regimented was the one thing that really alienated and depressed Dan. So much so that he was taking a fist full of pills every day.

Chapter 3, Foster and Group Homes

The next Dan knew they moved him to a foster home in Visalia which they thought would be a step up for him. They had very different rules than in a group home and Dan only lasted ten days. They had to ask to use the bathroom, to eat or nearly everything...and what really turned Dan off were the filthy conditions in the place.

He complained to his probation officer who sent him to a cooler foster home where he lived for seventy five days. The host gave them more freedom, but all the pills made Dan bad tempered and disagreeable. He wished he could have had the wisdom then to calm down, because Dan was the smartest foster child in the home and may have had a chance to be adopted. Instead, they finally asked his probation officer to move him.

The worst part of all this was that no one ever visited Dan. The other kids often had visitors on Sundays. That was constantly on his mind and it drove him nuts. Why didn't his nice uncle in Chicago take him in so he would be like his sisters? It made him promise that he would prove everybody's lack of expectations of him wrong and to show them that he didn't need them anyway. It changed his outlook a lot. His feelings would never be the same again.

Just stick it out and think positively and be productive with your time, he kept reminding himself.

* * *

After the second Visalia foster home they sent Dan to a group home in Visalia where he stayed for seven dreadful months. The group home was run by a politically active owner who wanted everything done his Marine Corps regimented way. He was new at the foster home business and didn't like Dan's city slicker demeanor.

The four other kids in the Visalia group house were plotting against him and the staff was against him too. So, out of staff view he got jumped on and beaten by three different boys. They wanted him to humble himself and he just refused to do so. After that he fought back until they left him alone. He hated the place because of the annoying kids. By then he got used to the unfair circumstances, but the waiting game still drove him nuts.

On the other hand, the teachers at school liked him and he enjoyed that part of his stay. But at winter break he was confined to the house for three whole weeks and finally couldn't take anymore and went absent without approval for two weeks.

He knew nothing about the city, and being hungry on the streets was his worst fear. He was thinly dressed and at the higher elevation it was cold outdoors. He finally knocked on the door of a very nice hooker who gave him room for the night because he was so young.

Dan's nearest relative was his grandmother. On this occasion he managed to reach his uncle in Chicago who paid his bus ticket to Arizona to visit his granny. She was happy to see him until she heard that he was on the run and called the cops. They found out that he was a fugitive from California and took him into custody until they could extradite him back to California. However, they treated Dan with respect which gave him some comfort.

* * *

A week later, he was in the Kern County jail. For Dan, that was the worst kind of punishment he ever had. He was so closely confined that it really made him feel claustrophobic and brought out the worst in him. Unlike the cops in Arizona, the Kern County wardens treated him like trash and while he hated group physical exercise, he was forced to do so daily. The inmates were aggressive and unfriendly, frequently threatening to gang up on Dan.

Next they kept him in Juvenile Hall for a week. That was the worst kind of treatment he ever had to live through, because of being locked in a room by himself within a structure with many rules, forcing him to do physical exercises whether he liked it or not.

Dan was angry and felt like no one cared about him. The more he thought about it, the more depressed he became. He hated everyone for being stuck in a system where nobody cared about him.

With better luck, he could have ended up in the care of a nice private family, but that was not to happen. You don't decide who you get. You just take your best choice to get out of the system as soon as possible.

Dan really didn't have such a bad record. It's just that there were different expectations in the minds of persons looking to adopt someone.

* * *

From there they sent him way up north on the road to Yosemite Park to a group home in Mariposa, where he lasted five weeks. He was on their football team, and even if he was better at the game than his opponents, the coach would never let him start, so he had to sit and wait, never to be called. He did this to spite Dan, because he was a city slicker from Bakersfield.

Dan exercised his rights, which got him into trouble with the owners. When he threatened to report them to the licensing board, they threw me out and he landed back in Bakersfield Juvenile Hall for another three whole weeks.

Chapter 4, Camp Owens

By then Dan was obviously viewed as a lost cause, because next they shipped him up to Camp Owens for three months. This was a home of a very different kind up in the mountains near Lake Isabella.

It was a hard labor camp for over a hundred incorrigible teenagers rebelling against society, being forced to work hard for long hours. Many of them were of Mexican descent and they divided themselves into Northern and Southern gangs who fought each other in a tradition that had been going on since the ninety sixties.

They made you get up very early and after being fed they made the inmates line up three to a row to relieve themselves. Sitting three feet apart, they had to empty their bowls with only six feet of tissue to wipe themselves. Then they were marched off for a day's hard labor in various disciplines in different groups.

They all showered together after working on the farm seven days a week and then they were made to sit on their beds for hours to get behavior points.

* * *

For Dan, the worst part was that they didn't see the inside of a proper school for three months, which was the only thing that kept him sane. The Kern High School District provided four teachers and three aides to teach English language arts, math, science and social studies.

All Dan got were three hours of schooling each week-day. Part of the problem was that most of the inmates arriving at the Camp were two grades below the average educational level for their age.

Counseling was available for anger and aggression management, substance abuse, and grief.

They provided for vocational training in janitorial work, landscaping, plumbing, welding, agriculture, animal husbandry and auto mechanics. Dan mostly worked at maintaining the hogs.

Some people enjoyed having something specific to do, but Dan was so angry about being held against his will that he didn't.

The only way he could endure was to remember how much worse it had been to be locked up in Juvenile Hall before coming to Camp Owens.

The Camp was operated on a behavior and achievement awards system. Each new arrival was evaluated as a personal risk and assigned 360 to 720 points. Based upon one's Camp behavior, school performance, homework completion, work performance and related actions. Points were deducted from the assigned risk level for good performance, or added for poor performance. If you achieved zero points, you theoretically could be released, but he didn't remember it happening to anyone while he was there.

Dan was always well below the average level, but the inmates were pretty rebellious and fights would frequently break out between factions until the guards moved in to break up the fights and lock them down. These gang-related problems added 100 points to each of their scores plus they were subject to disciplinary action.

Visitation was permitted on Sundays, but no one ever came to see Dan. Ever since he put foot in the foster care system, none of his family bothered to visit him.

The only outside interest he received was from the Rotary Club which sponsored a dinner once a month to honor inmates that had done well and he was singled out on one such occasion.

Chapter 5, The Bakersfield Group Home.

The owners of the Bakersfield group home appeared to be wealthy. They drove late model Jaguar and a Mercedes cars and lived in a fancy home while the five inmates were treated poorly and given very few resources.

The staff beat Dan a few times, but that was nothing in comparison with what the four foster boys did to him. They were pretty dumb and pretended to be a hardcore gang.

They didn't like Dan because he wouldn't allow himself to be intimidated by them, so they plotted behind his back. He could see what was coming. They ambushed him and beat him up pretty badly. They tried this stint on him several times until he fought back and slowly gained their respect, but never a glimmer of friendship.

* * *

Once Dan was settled in the Bakersfield group house he went to Bakersfield High School where he loved being. The teachers treated him with respect...like a human being. He studied hard and paid attention to get high marks in all the right subjects. It also helped that by then his acne had cleared up.

Even in that last group house, they still had to ask them to unlock the bathroom to use it! Dan finally could hardly take staying in a house all day where he got jumped and had his clothes stolen.

He wanted to go absent without leave because of the rules, and the rules were getting worse. So he just had to tolerate the place and what they were doing to him to get his high school units.

Dan had made up his mind, come what may, he was going to graduate from High School while he was still seventeen.

He wanted to graduate early and just stayed to get his credits. So Dan had to stick it out through the summer vacation, because if he ran away they would send him to Juvenile Hall where they didn't want people to tag with pencil tips, so there would be nothing to write with.

The reason he made enemies was because he usually was the role model of his unit and the kids that got into trouble were jealous and didn't like him for that.

His purgatory was to be confined to the group home during school holidays. It was like being in solitary confinement, with those four lousy boys in the poor house. His saving grace was that some of the staff members liked and treated him well.

Dan was rewarded by graduating from high school as he turned seventeen and could move on to junior college where he turned eighteen and was summarily tossed me out onto the street. There were no transition facilities of any kind.

Considering that he attended over twelve schools during his foster years, Dan was proud to make it into junior college before he was liberated.

The shame of it was that it had cost the taxpayers all of forty thousand dollars each year that he was confined!

As intelligent people it still baffles Dan that America can't do better with its kids.

Chapter 6, A Feminine Experience.

My parents used to drink and do drugs and moved from place to place, not ever having a real home. By the time I was seven I had still not set foot in a school and really didn't know right from wrong. I had three older sisters.

Then we went homeless and on a day when my parents had left us alone in a friend's apartment, child protective services came and took my older sister and me to a place called Jamison Center in Bakersfield where there were many children waiting to be dealt with. In no time at all, we were both infected with head lice.

My two older sisters in their mid-teens escaped, were later found, but soon again escaped.

They tried to give my sister and me some time in school, but since I couldn't even read or write, it didn't do much good, and besides, the place was a bit chaotic with bewildered children milling around, coming and going.

After about three months, child custody services finally placed my sister and me in a foster home at four thousand feet in the mountains around Tehachapi. My foster mother's name was Sarah and besides us, she had two other foster girls. She was single and a bit stressed-out with a short temper. She would beat us if we didn't keep our rooms spotlessly clean.

I had never been potty trained by my parents, which is what had kept me from going to school. This failed to endear me to my new foster mom.

We had been there about a month, when she really came at me during dinner, and almost as a reflex, I tossed a butter knife at her. That was it, and we were forced to leave.

* * *

Our next home was with really nice parents who loved us at first sight and we thought they were going to be our parents forever. We had classes every day and if we were good, we could get to play on the playground. Then custody services brought new kids who replaced us and we were taken back to Jamison Center.

Our real parents wanted us back, but the social workers wouldn't let them have us. We were too young to understand what was going on.

* * *

I was about eight years old when we were placed into our next foster home where we lived for four years.

They made us feel as though they were our real family and treated us gently and with respect. They had a much older daughter who lived elsewhere with her sixteen year old son. She visited her parents frequently and we got to know her well.

Once, when they were visiting, her son came into my room in the middle of the night, climbed into bed with me and touched me in ways I had not experienced. Before I knew what was happening, he forced himself upon me to have intercourse. I had no concept of the feelings it provoked within me and it scared me out of my wits. I knew that we had broken very important rules and could never bring myself to tell anyone about it.

By the time I was twelve, our foster mom and dad decided to retire and with the approval of the foster care officials they moved us to their daughter's home. We loved their daughter and all was well for the next year except that I had a falling out with my sister who kept blaming me for putting us into foster care, while she still loved our rotten parents. It got so bad that they moved her to a different foster home.

My real grandma would write me letters, but I never received what she included in her letters. My foster mom must have kept it for some reason.

One night my foster mom left to go to a party. I had gone to bed early and woke up to find her son on top of me. He put his hand over my mouth so no one could hear and warned me that if I told anyone he would kill me. He then did to me what he had done before and said that if I was nice to him he would do it to me more often. I was dead scared and submitted to him until it seemed like a normal, somewhat pleasing thing to experience.

A year later, he raped another foster girl who called the police. They came and took all of us foster kids away from the home.

I had nowhere to go until my sister's foster mother decided to take me in. So in sixth grade I was back together with my sister. The first two years I lived there with her, I seldom spoke because I was scared that someone would find out about me having sex with my previous mom's boy. The only way I communicated was to shake my head to say yes or no.

I was finally diagnosed to be suffering from posttraumatic stress disorder caused by harboring my fears and secret shameful affinities.

I was thirteen by then and was put into special classes for kids lagging behind their class levels. They taught me how to read and write and gave me speech training. Through counseling and therapy I also began to improve by the time I turned fourteen.

Over time I began to reconcile myself with my buried sexual desires which I never brought to light with any of my councilors and compensated for by seriously engaging in sports.

My greatest motivation was <u>not</u> to grow up to be like my parents.

By the time I was eighteen I opted to continue living with my foster mom as my legal mother.

I made it through the foster care system as did my sister, who is married and has a daughter who I dearly love. We lost touch with our birth mother and father and our older sisters who all still live under a cloud of liquor and drug addiction.

As for my silent sex drive, I am engaged to a U.S. Marine who greatly enjoys that side of me as I approach graduation from college in the hopes of joining the police force.

Chapter 7, Dreadful Feminine Experience

My sister and I were taken away from our family when I was three and she was four. My father had committed suicide and my grieving mother took to drinking and taking drugs. We and our baby brother were essentially living with our grandparents when, because of the presence of our addicted mother, child protective services took us into custody and placed us into foster care.

Judy, our foster mother in a small town north of Bakersfield, had lots of hang-ups and didn't accept us well. She did as little as possible for us, while maintaining the income she received for keeping us. There were two of her family's boys living there who she treated extremely well in sharp contrast with how she treated us. We were not allowed to celebrate Christmas, even to the point of her taking the presents our grandfather brought us away as soon as he left to give them to her relatives.

Two years later, protective child services added our little brother to the foster household. When we reached school age our foster mother was bound by law to let us attend school and while I don't remember much about those years, I have pictures of us taken at several schools.

We were often beaten for minimal reasons, even a silly remark as a kid would make. I remember being beaten repeatedly on my head with a bat that hung over the headboard of her 32 year old son.

* * *

By the time my sister and I were in middle school, the beatings got so bad that our school teacher had to call the police because of the bruises my sister and I had sustained. The police took photographs of our injuries and when we got home we were berated by Judy and relegated to be home schooled. We shared the same homeschool teacher for two hours with each of us on weekdays and kept notes of what she told each of us so we could cure my sister's inability to keep up with her class. After the teacher left, we worked from the notes of what she had told each of us.

There were other forms of punishment and I vividly remember when I was around 7 or 8 when they forced me to stand in a corner until my legs wouldn't hold me anymore and then threw golf balls at my head.

What I found most grievous was when our foster mother's 32 year old son, who was not legally entitled to be there, raped both me and my sister, and continued to force us to have sex with him repeatedly. By the time we were in sixth grade, they found him molesting his own four year old son and took him off to prison.

* * *

One day when I was about 11 we were abruptly taken to the trailer park where our grandparents lived and told to find our way to their home. I stayed there until I went to live with my boyfriend's parents after I got pregnant.

My mom got me started on meth at the age of 13. The first time I did drugs I passed out and didn't wake up for 3 days. I was on Meth for a year, and quit when I found out at 14 that I was two weeks pregnant with my first child.

When I gave birth to my baby my boyfriend was on probation which he violated, so they were looking for him. They went to his mother's home where we were staying to find him and since he had taken flight, they took my baby daughter and told us in order to get her back he had to turn himself in.

He refused to do so and I went down to the child protective services office to see what I could do to get my child back. My brother went with me. They found out that we weren't living with, Judy, the evil monster, anymore. So they took both my brother and me back into foster care. I went through three different foster care places before I could get my baby back.

* * *

When I was 16 my mother committed suicide in a grubby motel room. It really left me feeling hurt, abandoned and lost, even though, considering her condition, I felt relieved. But that's when I went back to doing drugs and ended up having my baby taken away again. I ran away from the group home and was on drugs for about six to seven months when I they arrested me for child abandonment and locked me up in Juvenile Hall for almost 2 months. After that they sent me to a group home in Mariposa to be cured of my drug habit.

It took a whole year to pass the group home's test for sobriety, after which I was allowed to go back to a Bakersfield group home. I lived there for another year to satisfy them that I was cured, before they gave my daughter back to me.

By the time I was eighteen and left foster care to live with my sister, I discovered that our erstwhile foster care mother had indeed been collecting payment for keeping us for all the years after she had dropped us off at the trailer park. None of the case workers ever checked on us when we lived there and they obviously didn't check the group-home later either.

While I was with my sister, I fell in love with my future husband and moved away to Georgia where we were married and I gave birth to my second daughter. He ran off with another woman and I had to return to Bakersfield with my two daughters. He was into drugs and before long he was unable to pay me for child support. He left me struggling to get baby care for the little one while my first born is at pre-school, so I can find a job.

Note:

She has since called to say that she has secured a job, but then later had to move because of gangsters murdering people next door to her and her kids. It's a hard life to sustain oneself along with two children, one an infant and the other in pre-school. She is planning to marry a young man from Idaho.

Chapter 8, A Most Unusual Feminine Experience

When my twin sister and I were fourteen, we lived next door to a very kind widower. His wife had suddenly died from a serious stroke. He had a very nice garden with a large swimming pool where my year older sister and my twin and I used to swim after school. He wrote books and had his office on the ground floor of his home. He sometimes sat outside and often brought out a thermos flask of cold fruit juice with plastic cups for us to use. We called him Mr. A.

My dad had lost his job and try as he may, nothing came along. He even tried doing part time work, which helped, but came nowhere near covering our living costs. So my mother also took various jobs, from being a sales lady in department stores, to being a secretary to the owner of a construction company. She put in many hours and really appreciated Mr. A for keeping an eye on us after school. Other than that we didn't know much about him.

As months went by, my dad became increasingly irritable and unkind to us, making demands and expecting us to jump to attention to obey him. Some of his cronies would come over with booze when they had nothing better to do and he gradually became a drunk.

As much as possible, my sisters and I stayed clear of him and his cronies while our mom was at work, but we couldn't stay over at Mr. A's house without dad noticing and then he would beat us. He used a whip with many tails which stung, but didn't leave obvious marks on our legs.

Then one day when our sister gave him lip, he undressed and raped her. He made her stand on her hands and knees in front of him and then poked her mercilessly. He made her swear that she would never tell our mother what he was doing to her.

When he discovered that my twin and I knew what was happening, he started to come after us too. The temptation to tell Mr. A how we were being abused was just too much for my twin who is more outgoing than I am and she wound up telling Mr. A. He began leaving lights on at night so we could escape if necessary.

Then one evening three of dad's worst cronies came over and before he let them into the house I heard him ask them if they had brought the money with them. They came into the house and almost immediately two of them grabbed my older sister, tore her clothes off and one of the men began raping her while the other one made her take him into her mouth. Alerted by the commotion, Mr. A came crashing through the patio door. As the third man jumped at him he ducked his punch and with the momentum the man had, made him crash into the fireplace wall. As he struggled to get up Mr. A folded one leg over the other and put huge force on the upper leg to dislocate his knee.

The two men raping my sister turned on him, but they were no match for Mr. A, who obviously must have had martial arts training and moments later they too were immobilized. He prevailed on my speechless mother to call 911 while he and my older sister tied them up with rope and plastic ties which he sent me to fetch from his garage.

The cops took the bad guys away and searched their car which was full of gangster paraphernalia, including hand guns with their serial numbers filed off. They questioned my dad who tried to excuse himself until my sharp-tongued twin, who they interviewed, blurted out how he had taken advantage of us three girls. Then they took him away and put him in a holding cell. They also took Mr. A and my sister with them. In her case they wanted DNA samples to incriminate the two gangsters who had raped her.

From Mr. A they wanted to know why he appeared on the scene and how he had become so good at martial arts. It turned out that he had served in the Marine Corps.

Since the door into our home had been destroyed, we all went over to Mr. A's place for the night. We three girls were given Mr. A's bedroom with an extra fold up bed added.

My mother stayed downstairs to talk to Mr. A. According to our older sister, he wanted to know how she could have remained silent when she knew that my dad was forcing us to have sex with him. I had wondered about that many times and couldn't believe that she kept quiet just out of fear. She had lots of opportunity from her place of work to call the cops, or at least someone in social services.

Instead of raking her over the coals Mr. A sought to understand her position. Thinking back now, I can see what he was trying to do. He wanted to keep us together as a family for a purpose. Perhaps he thought he could somehow bring my dad back into the family and that really frightened me.

Unlike my two sisters who wore their hearts on their sleeves, I had real trouble even thinking of staying anywhere near my dad. He used to be such a good, loving dad, until he turned into a rogue, for which I could never forgive him.

A few days later they had a court hearing and since my twin and I were under the age of sixteen, my dad was sent to jail for having sex with minors. I breathed a sigh of relief, but remained deeply concerned about what would happen to us.

* * *

When we got home from school at Mr. A's house, he was over at our house, fixing the door he had kicked in and since everybody was busy doing their own chores I sneaked over to talk to him.

I asked him what was going to happen to us.

He said that he wasn't certain and asked me not to mention it to the others yet, but that he was considering becoming our foster parent in spite of being a single man.

I asked him what would happen to my mom, since she tolerated the abuse of her girls.

He didn't know the answer since she was still married to my dad and that she would have to stay in her own house to begin with.

I told him that my dad's behavior created serious emotional problems for me and that I doubted that I could trust any man again.

He said that we would have to get professional help for all three of us girls.

I asked him why he didn't just adopt us as his own children so we could feel safe and free of care.

He said that the adoption process had become so complicated that we would come of age before that could be approved. Also, he wasn't sure that his application wouldn't trigger us to be taken into foster care, unless we could prove that my mother would take good care of us.

He then asked me what I thought of my mom.

I had to confess that we thought she had betrayed us and that he had to understand what it was like to be sexually violated by one's own father.

I also told him that my older sister was deeply in love with him and would most likely try to seduce him.

If that happened, he said, it would have to be consensual sex and not rape, since she is over sixteen and he wouldn't do it unless it was absolutely necessary for her well-being. He asked me to think what I would feel like if those two vile men had done to me what they were doing to my sister when he came on the scene?

I asked him what if I felt the same way.

He thought for a long time before answering. He said that it would be illegal and that his purpose was to give us a happy, secure home and not a harem.

I asked him one more time, saying that what my father did to me revolted me so deeply, that I would always be frigid when it came to sex.

He said that I was putting him on the spot, and that it would take an experienced psychoanalyst to draw that conclusion.

That was enough encouragement for me and when we saw how gentle he was, we all championed his foster home application until it was approved.

We each had our own bedroom and Mr. A was quite strict about us keeping them clean and tidy. That was a problem for my scatterbrain twin and I found it interesting to see the patient way he had of bringing her into line. All three of us shared the upstairs bathroom, leaving the ground floor as our living quarters and for Mr. A's study and his bathroom.

He was very thoughtful and always had entertaining work programs set up for us, including physical exercise which included long bike rides for which each of us, including our mother, was given a good road bike.

There was no question that we all loved him and that he treaded us as if we were his own children. He was wide open to discussing any problem we encountered, which included the subject of being raped by our dad. My twin was very outspoken on that subject and after many deliberations between our social worker from foster care and my mother it was decided to seek professional trauma help.

In the meantime Mr. A enlisted us in ballroom dancing classes for which we all had the right kind of figures. Our older sister loved to be dramatic and it wasn't long before Mr. A and she set the pace by dancing the Tango, as if they were in Buenos Aires. The teacher encouraged them by entering them in local competitions which they won hands down.

That set the tone and I specialized in dancing the waltz, which was more quietly dramatic to suit my character. I loved feeling his body enmeshed with mine and we went all out to win my part of the contest.

My more dramatic twin went for perfecting the Charleston, the Cha Cha and Rhumba. The consensus was that she excelled in doing the Rhumba, whereas I liked her Charleston best.

Our mother excelled in doing the Foxtrot and the Bossa Nova.

It didn't make much sense to be living in two adjacent homes and Mr. A launched a program to rehabilitate our old house. We were each given assignments that tied together as a team effort. At first my older sister and my twin balked at the idea, but were soon talked into it when it became a race to win prizes. We were cleaning and helping him move furniture, while he focused on fixing electrical wiring, plumbing and lighting before moving outdoors to mow the overgrown lawns, prune trees and bushes, and mend fences. It took all of three weeks before it ended in the garage of our old house, which turned up a font of photographs and memorabilia.

My mother's divorce from my dad came through and Mr. A negotiated a settlement for the property with my dad who would be in jail for many more years.

The negotiation with the foster care people to allow my mother to move into the main house was far more complicated. They were still uncomfortable, as was I, about her quiescence in not blowing the whistle on my dad when he began messing with us. In the end they agreed only to allow her to live in a small apartment adjacent to Mr. A's garage which was briefly used by his deceased wife's grandmother, before she passed away. They then leased our old home to a family with children.

* * *

The school year came to an end and Mr. A decided to take us to a place on the shore near Virginia Beach, hoping that we could see the horses come ashore from Chincoteague Island, which they do once a year.

We had our camping gear with us and practically lived on the beach. That was the first time I noticed signs of a relationship developing between Mr. A and my older sister. She was very mature for her age, after all the horrible things that had happened to her, and since he had entered the house just in time to release her from the two dreadful men, she must have felt some kind of obligation to him because she was the aggressor romancing him and he was the reluctant participant.

I had the advantage of verbal communication with Mr. A and took him aside to ask him. He responded simply saying that my sister saw her savior in him and that she was bowled over by his aggressive defense of her, causing her to fall madly in love with him. He asked me what I would have done under her circumstances.

I told him that we all felt that way about him. He seemed genuinely flattered, but came back to the subject of my sister. He said that if he failed to respond to her she was in dire danger of losing all self-respect and given her intellect, charm and capability it left him no choice in the matter.

His conclusion astounded me, but the stark reality of his reasoning was undeniable. He added that there was no one-upmanship in her demeanor and that she was exclusively driven by her overwhelming love for him. He was almost in tears as he spoke, and I knew that he meant every word of it.

I love my sister without reservation as does my twin and we would just have to find a way to live with it. In my twin's opinion, there was nothing illegal about him marrying our sister, who was approaching her seventeenth birthday. The only question lay in how the foster care people would respond to it.

That evening she slipped into his tent and they spent the night together. I had never seen her as radiant and happy as she appeared the next day. I questioned her and she said that he made love to her very gently and with so much concern for her greatest comfort and enjoyment that it blotted away her images of that terrible night. She said they simply made love to each other in every possible way, and that none of it felt crude or obscene.

I thought we would see very little of him outside of her company, but he never let that happen.

By the end of our stay on the beach we went to see the horses swim ashore at Chincoteague Island. We watched men on horseback round up more than a hundred ponies on Assateague Island and fifty more from the southern end and herd them into two corrals. We were there by six in the morning to wait for the tide to turn when for a short while at around eleven o'clock there was no tide when they herded the horses to swim across.

The vacation trip really brought us together in a way we had never experienced and for a change we were happy to start the new school term.

* * *

The time had come to meet with the trauma expert. We were happy in our new environment, but unlike my older sister, my twin and I still had psychological problems stemming from being raped repeatedly by our dad.

The expert questioned us in great detail and came to the conclusion that we needed a positive experience to offset our fears of experiencing a wrong sexual event. While she questioned each of us separately, my twin and I silently came to the same conclusion that what had worked for our sister would also liberate us from our fears.

She had provided us with videos that explained the physical aspects of inducing a satisfying orgasm, which had some revealing value which we tried on ourselves and on each other with limited success.

We decided that Mr. A could solve our problems in the same way he had turned our sister into a model of happiness. I was deputized to convince him that we could feign great success with the process prescribed by the trauma expert if he would agree to make love to us.

He listened intently to my argument, in the course of which I embraced and kissed him suggestively. I was certain that he found both of us physically attractive and that it would be no skin off his nose if he made love to us. His concern was more that we would try to make it into a habit and that he couldn't live up to such expectations. It was clear that he was seriously in love with our sister and would probably marry her when she turned eighteen, or sooner if they could get away with it without challenging our foster care standing.

He asked for a conference between all three of us, also attended by our mother. Her stake in our communal existence was that she too craved his attention and wanted a more profound role in our family life. To my surprise, my twin stepped forward with a most compelling rationale to have him become our mentor in putting the past horrors behind us. She was even careful to respect my mother's ambiguous position for not having blown the whistle on our erstwhile dad.

That unexpected diplomacy, more than anything else, seemed to do more to convince him, and he agreed to teach us how to make love in a magnanimous way. We drew straws and my twin became the lead in our endeavor.

To set the stage, he once again tried to imbue us with the art of truly loving each other...that it had to be as selfless as possible and very passionate with great respect for the pleasure of both parties involved. The spirit and the flesh had to be in complete harmony so that no activity could be considered lewd.

Just listening made me love him even more than I already did. The upside was that he had seemingly captured the wayward side of my sister as well.

Each of us would have dinner with him in a relaxed setting before spending the night with him in reasonable opulence. My older sister would take charge of our wardrobe for each occasion. I greatly admired her selflessness for being so forthcoming, knowing how desperately she loved him. Her taste in clothes was impeccable and my twin left on her date looking ravishing.

She was in high spirits when she came home the next morning with a spring in her step again. She wouldn't elaborate since she had promised Mr. A not to influence me. All she would say was that her adverse reaction to the idea of sexual intercourse no longer existed.

My outfit when my turn came was designed to make me look more of a vamp than I really am, but in retrospect my twin didn't need embellishment either. I was as nervous as a scared cat when we left home. Knowing what I was going through he calmed me down by telling me a funny story about a woman who had also watched the swimming of the horses to Chincoteague Island and had fallen into the water from a dock chasing after her Golden Retriever which decided to join the horses. The problem was that she couldn't swim and he had to jump in to save her.

We were served dinner in a candle-lit private dining room which he explained was designed to make me vividly remember the occasion. He said that this evening had to stand out so much in my mind's eye that anything bad in the past would be minimized if not forgotten. He wanted me to reach my full potential in life, which in his estimation was very large.

By the time we reached our hotel suite I was totally relaxed and put my arms around his neck to kiss him passionately. He responded in kind and we kissed each other without inhibitions. He gently undressed me as we continued kissing each other until I was totally naked.

He obviously liked what he was seeing and began fondling my breasts with his hands and taking them into his mouth. The night turned into a blissful time of highly satisfying experiences, which he characterized as the very least I should expect from any man that I would consider for a permanent relationship. He gave me a ruby adorned ring in remembrance of the occasion.

I certainly had no sexual inhibitions left in me when we checked out and went home.

I was beaming when my sister welcomed me back into the family fold.

Our final meeting with the trauma expert was very successful and we passed her examination with flying colors.

Mr. A married my sister when she turned eighteen and they had their first child while my twin and I we were still his foster children. Our greatest challenges were to qualify our boyfriends to be admitted to his home. By then our tastes in suitable men had become quite sophisticated as we planned our respective ways into higher education. My twin sister and I always remained in love with this gentle man who gave so much of himself to us, even when it was illegal for him to do so.

The foster care people prevailed on Mr. A and my sister to take in foster children, which they agreed to do as long as they were still young, malleable kids. I went on to an academic career in health services and my twin sister studied drama and started acting in stage plays.

We are both engaged to men who had struggled hard and long to meet the criteria set for them by our foster dad.

Chapter 9, Humane Foster Care Approaches

According to an Idaho couple, who work for the Idaho, *Division of Children and Family Services*, their state with a population of 1.5 million people, has approximately 1,600 kids in foster care. Unlike California with county-managed foster care, Idaho has a state run system with more consistency and greater efficiency. Our couple works with foster youth and foster families on a daily basis.

California has experienced huge budget issues with local government staff reductions. Idaho works year to year with a balanced budget per its state constitution and has not experienced staff reductions. The couple acknowledges that their dealings with California's child welfare system often yield unpleasant results.

They point out the difference between foster care issues and those affecting foster care children who are also guilty of criminal offenses. Kids in foster care are in care because their caregivers cannot provide a safe and stable home environment for them. Foster care children in the criminal justice system should expect to be punished.

Idaho actively works with caregivers to open avenues to get the kids back home with their natural parents as quickly as possible, since the primary goal always remains the reunification of the family.

In addition, Idaho places more than half of its foster kids with relatives such as grandparents, aunts, uncles and nephews, on the theory that relatives have greater interest in the welfare of the children than strange foster parents may have.

Criminal inmates who may also be foster children have been remanded to the custody of the juvenile or adult correction system and have to fulfill their punishment for criminal conduct. That can be a brutal experience especially in a gang infested state like California.

No doubt there are foster parents who miss-use the money they are given. In the experience of the couple being quoted, that is a rare exception in Idaho where social workers keep a pretty close watch on the kids in care as well as their foster parents.

Another Idaho advantage is that it has very few group homes for kids in foster care. The typical Idaho foster home consists of a normal family home and they are frequently visited and regularly given help to solve problems.

Chapter 10, The Foster/Adoption Alternative.

Infertile mothers often consider fostering a child with the intention of adopting it as their own. We spoke to one such mother who wanted to take a nine month old baby boy as a foster child while at the same time applying to adopt him.

She immediately found herself in the hands of a county foster child bureaucracy while at the same time being at the mercy a state adoption agency. In her case, the boy had been taken from his drug addicted parents who had physically abused him. Nevertheless, under California law she had to wait for eighteen months to give his parents a fair chance at mending their ways in order to reclaim him, before the adoption process could proceed.

There always exists a dichotomy between well intentioned parents wishing to clean up their act, and those principally interested in the material benefits they could get, without mending their ways.

In this case, in addition to addiction, it also involved the lack of anger management, which resulted in a head injury to the baby and precipitated his removal. He was placed as the 26th baby into the care of a seasoned foster mother. She provided strictly adequate care, but with almost no expression of love in her correct mechanical methods.

She would wake him early, change his diaper and leave him sitting in his cradle until she was ready to bathe him at around nine, and so his day continued with specific events without any socializing. The woman aiming to adopt him characterized this as boarding house management.

The head wound he had suffered had healed satisfactorily and once the paperwork from the adoption and foster care agencies had been approved the child was turned over to the woman we interviewed.

She was relieved because regardless of malfeasance, some guilty parents would attempt to physically abduct their child from its foster parent. To avoid that possibility, foster care case workers have the ability to sometimes move a child to an unknown foster care address.

Since foster care in California is a county responsibility, there are borderline cases where case workers from two different counties, equally perplexed by the lack of foster care spaces, will place children in the same facility not knowing what the other case worker had done. This results in crowding facilities beyond their reasonable capacities with up to four children sharing one small room.

The San Joaquin Valley north of Fresno is a largely rural agricultural domain and case workers face driving as far as fifty miles to reach some of the foster homes. This detracts from the thoroughness of their supervision. To mitigate this problem our adopting mother favored oversight by independent agents, preferably at the state level.

This type of overcrowding leads to gang formation and can result in the violent death of inmates. In Los Angeles inner city schools, for instance, the presence of gangs is so prevalent that their school systems sometimes need to extend danger pay to their teachers.

The State of California stages annual picnics in various locations to bring the public and foster children together, with the objective of promoting the adoption of some of the children. It was obvious to our prospective mother during her period of uncertain outcome, that the public participants at these picnics were principally interested in adopting very young children.

According to her, the consensus appeared to be that children beyond the age of four may already have suffered too much damage to adopt. In her opinion many of the older foster children would be far better off living on their own with funding support from the counties rather than to be kept in foster homes. In the end they have to make that transition anyway and in her opinion starting it earlier would be to everyone's advantage.

Once her ten month old foster/adoption baby was in her possession she could start the process of instilling love and affection in his soul. This proved to be a slow process in which he could barely tolerate riding in a car for any length of time. One such occasion was when the entire California branch of the family trekked out in a convoy to a clan gathering in Colorado, coordinating stops by CB radio. The youngster stayed conscious the entire eighteen hours and refused to sleep.

He gradually began to respond to her affection and by the time the possible assumption of adoption came, he was close to normal expectations. Observing his cautious behavior, led her to believe that foster parents needed to check on the children in their care more often. School teachers agreed with her, saying that they almost routinely have to notify law enforcement of signs of abuse.

While the attempts of the parents of her son-to-be were not on solid ground, they nevertheless tried to regain possession in order to milk foster care for the financial assistance they thought would come with him. Fortunately the state and county saw through their ruse and approved her adoption of the child.

He is now nearing his 18th birthday and has become a good son even though he still prefers his own company which he enjoys as a cross-country bike racer. He has healthy aspirations to lead a successful life, but still has a lot to learn about managing his own financial affairs.

* * *

Unlike her adopted son, those who had been removed from their families because of maltreatment, leave foster care because of their age and not because of achieving a certain standard of self-reliance. The state cannot connect them to a permanent legal family and they are left on their own to find a support network to meet their legal, emotional, psychological, and cultural needs.

In today's society, young people may not become self-sufficient adults until well after the age at which they leave foster care. They need to depend on others for emotional and tangible support until they have sufficient education and/or training to obtain a decent job, support themselves, and establish their own homes and families.

This is a process that normally begins at childhood and continues into the teen years and beyond. They don't learn key life skills, such as learning to manage money and making independent decisions, until after they leave foster care to move into adulthood. That is where family life would normally provide emotional, social, and material support.

Without strong, stable connections to other significant adults, those leaving foster care are left on their own to face their own key developmental decisions. As they approach the age of majority, they must make the transition to adulthood without family support, with fewer financial resources, and without the safety net most other young people enjoy.

Study after study shows that, as a group, these young people fare poorly as they attempt to negotiate the world of adulthood.

For example, Ventura County with a population of about 830,000 has around 800 children in foster care at any one time.

- 83% of these foster children are held back by the third grade.
- 46% of them do not complete high school.
- 70% of emancipating teens report that they want to attend college, but fewer than 10% of those who graduate from high school enroll in college. Less than 1% graduate from college.

Ventura foster children as a group compared with their peers:

- Function at lower academic levels,
- Exhibit more behavioral problems, and
- Experience higher rates of mental illness

Upon emancipation from foster care:

- 65% of them need immediate housing,
- 40-50% become homeless within 18 months, and
- 25% of them will be incarcerated within two years of emancipation!

The foster population density in Los Angeles and Kern counties per thousand inhabitants are twice as high as in Ventura County and even more so in San Bernardino County.

The system is clearly inadequate and in need of a major overhaul, in California, also including the modernization of archaic family laws.

Chapter 11, New Jersey Female Rebel

My mother suffered from a bi-polar disorder and ever since I was 10 years old, I found it impossible to live with her. So I began crashing with friends and at times going homeless. I then found some rewarding things to do, like delivering express messages and documents by bicycle, through Manhattan's frequently snarled traffic.

I also misbehaved as I explored every new sensation that came to mind. My father had taken off and for several years I had no idea where he was. By the time I was 13, child protection services confined me to a stream of state or charity-run boarding schools and group homes.

My behavior was uncontrollable and I pursued all possible means to escape servitude such as sliding down laundry shoots to the outside world. I just couldn't stand having people constantly intruding into my private space.

While staying in a converted YMCA in New Jersey, I overdosed on alcohol and lost consciousness for several days with a serious case of alcohol poisoning. I was left in a backroom without any assistance to recover. After that I was a bad, promiscuous kid seeking the company of badly behaved kids until they confined me to New Jersey lockups in New Brunswick and in Elizabeth.

The punitive measures in those places were severe, bordering on prison levels. I rebelled against it as much as possible. My most prized possessions were my drawings and artwork which they threatened to burn, unless I agreed to rat on someone else, which I absolutely would not do.

One of the counselors really had it in for me and militated in favor of sending me to a correctional facility in Texas. She came close to succeeding on two occasions and would have done so, had it not been for my probation officer who went to bat for me.

During the hearings my mother testified against me, but the combination of my own articulate arguments and my probation officer's testimony got me exonerated, and at age 16 I was released on my own cognizance and went to live with my older brother for a while and then moved in with my mother's mother.

In overall perspective, I was uncontrollable, didn't like intrusion, and preferred to live by my own rules or simply walk away. There was a lot of violence amongst the inmates. I haven't thought about it for a long time and even now it hurts me to remember some of it. One group home had its own resident school which was a big mistake in my opinion. My escapes usually ended in being confined to Juvenile Hall.

That was every bit like being in prison and I still find it too personal to talk about. Given her own emotional problems, my mother was sadistic in her opposition to me.

When I was 18, I moved to Manhattan to become involved in nightclub management and ultimately became the marketing manager for the Palladium, which in the 1990's was the best attended night club in New York City.

By then I had acquired a degree in film production and marketing which finally drew me to Hollywood. I was nearing the end of my child bearing age and since I didn't want the intrusion of a male companion in my life, I had myself inseminated and now have my own very talented daughter.

If I had to describe myself in a single word, it would be INDEPENDENT and definitely a misfit in any foster care system.

Chapter 12, Mentally Impaired in Foster Care

This narrative was composed by a close family member with the language skills our subject lacks.

My childhood was spent in the foster care system which I entered when I was seven. Throughout my childhood and teenage years, I was in many foster care and group home placements. In retrospect, it was a mixture of good and bad experiences.

The most difficult part of foster-care is the uncertainty of one's existence. There is always a sense of the unknown and confusion about the future. It makes one feel afraid and alone. It is hard for any child to go through foster care, but I had mental disabilities and could not understand what was going on in my life.

The only time I really remember was when the social worker came to our house to take us away. That was the last time we saw that case worker, because she never visited us in the foster home. It was important for me to know what was happening in my life. I needed someone to explain things to me in a way that I could understand...a person I could trust and talk to about things. Sometimes it felt like the foster homes were just in it for the money.

It felt like they did not care about me because I had a disability. In one foster home, the woman's son hurt me. When I told her what her son had done, she beat me for telling on him. If a case worker had come to the home, I would have told her about what had happened to me.

Being separated from my siblings was another painful part of foster care. I was the oldest in my family, followed by my brother and little sister. My brother and I were always placed in the same home, but my sister was always in a different foster home because most foster homes preferred to accept very young children. I always wondered about my kid sister...about what she was doing and if she missed me. It really hurt me to be away from her. It did not feel right being with strangers. I was always glad to go back to my mom. Living with my family always felt like the best thing for me.

When I was 13, a boy in the neighborhood took advantage of me, and I became pregnant. Because I was a child in foster care and an underage mom, I became a part of the child protection system in a new way.

As a parent, I felt that a lot of things I ran into with child protection were because I was a young mom with a disability. When child protection looked at me, it seemed to me they only saw my disability. I felt that they used my disability against me.

I was a good mom, and I took care of my son. I even graduated from a parenting skills program. I felt that I was doing all the right things, but they were still judging me. Even though I had done everything that I was supposed to do, they took my son away from me.

It would have been helpful to have someone supporting me, someone who knew me and knew how hard I was trying to be a good parent. It seemed that all they saw was my disability without looking further to see that I was a good mother.

Some of my experiences in foster care were positive. When I was eight years old, I was placed in a wonderful and nurturing foster home. This foster mom showed us love, patience, and kindness...all of the things a child needs. It felt like a real home to me. We each had household chores. I learned about cleaning, cooking, and laundry. She told me when I grew up I would have a family, and that I would be a good mom. It was very important to me that she took the time to listen and explain things in a way that I could understand. She talked to me about my own mother, and why she could not take care of us.

That was the first time I remember someone explaining things to me. She knew that I had a disability, but she made me feel that she understood what that was like. My disability made me feel badly about myself. I could not read, and I was behind all the other students. My classmates called me retarded and teased me about being in foster care. My foster mom said that I just learned differently, at a different pace. Because of her support, I started to see my disability in a better light.

When I became a teenager I made some bad choices and got into trouble. I was sent to a special school for disabled people like me. That experience changed my life. The staff members at the school were wonderful. They believed in me and cared about my future. My opinions were important to them. They even came to me for advice sometimes. It was the first time in my life that anyone seemed interested in my thoughts. It helped me to feel confident and to see that I had important things to share. It completely changed me and I give them credit for my success. The special educators understood my needs and abilities. They worked with me on my school work, and built up my self-esteem.

Because of this I learned to understand my experiences in foster care.

It seems wrong that throughout all those years in the child protection system, I never had a real relationship with any of my case workers. As a child with a disability, it was hard to have so much uncertainty and change. A relationship with my case worker could have provided me with some stability and helped me to be less afraid.

As a parent, I realized that I needed more support from the child protection system. Losing my son was one of the hardest things in my life. Later on, I had the opportunity to have him come back to live with me. He was so happy where he was living, that I did not want to take him away from it. It was hard to let him go, but I thought it was best for him. It still hurts me to know that things could have been different for us. I used to have a lot of anger towards my mother; now I know why she did what she did. It took me a long time to come to this understanding.

I am now the mother of four children, and having my own kids has taught me a lot about life. I used to say that when I have my own kids I do not want them to go through what I had to go through in my life. I do not want them to grow up in foster care.

The best place for them is with me, as a part of a family. They are the most important part of my life, and I want to be the best parent I can ever be. That is why I continue to take parenting classes and accept support. Most of all, I know now that even though I have a disability, I am a good wife and mother.

Chapter 13, A Successful Foster Home

Judy came from a large Wisconsin family presided over by her no-nonsense, Marine Corps father. After her own two daughters and three sons had grown up and were successfully established in their own careers, she decided to start a foster home on their farm near Racine.

I heard about her from her daughter in a chance meeting at a farmer's market in Ojai, California and called her.

She told me that she went to school to become qualified in the eyes of the state foster care authorities and opened her doors with two young foster daughters. She followed the family rules instilled in her by her father to persuade children in a non-confrontational manner to adhere to firmly set family rules which were based upon achievement, participation in sports, constructive contributions to the family and the absence of reliance on television and electronic media.

Two years into her twelve year stint as a foster home, the two young daughters were placed with reliable family members and Judy went on after the turn of the century to sustain a foster home with an average capacity of four to five foster children at one time of all ages.

She expected her foster children by age 12 to have a paying job of some kind and by age 18 they had to approach self-sufficiency, even though with the agreement of the state, she continued to house and mentor them for longer periods, if necessary.

Her deeply felt objective was not to foster losers and to send only self-sustaining young people out into the world. Many of them returned with pride periodically to show what they had accomplished with what she had taught them. They all felt as though they were part of her family and dearly loved her.

Newcomers were introduced kindly, but persistently into enjoying a healthy life style with lots of fruit and healthy diets along with enjoyable elements of competitive sports, nature outings, conscientious schooling and holding down a job. No television or cell phones were permitted. During the long winter months they sometimes made outings into the ski hills as a family diversion. Addiction to smoking was discouraged and terminated with more bananas in their diet to increase their intake of potassium.

Initiation of newcomers with mental debilitations such as attention deficiency syndrome, were slowly and patiently brought into the fold without being made to feel inferior. This became very time consuming in certain instances with new older children lacking any discipline in their backgrounds. She spent many hours encouraging such children without condemning their bad habits by pointing out the benefits of the alternative life style in her home.

In the end they invariably became her strongest supporters and many of them still pay her frequent visits.

Her relationships with the foster care administrators varied from good and appreciative to arrogant and dismissive of her home's achievements. If anything she felt that there was a tendency to downplay the importance of foster home contributions to the state system. This is belied by the fact that in some years foster parents became the adoptive parents in 82% of adoption cases in Wisconsin.

From talking to other foster parents, Judy stands out for the selfless, untiring effort she made to tackle her most challenging foster children, and by persuasion alone to bring them to a stage from which they could become successful and self-confident.

On a typical day in Wisconsin, a state of over 5.7 million, something less than 7,000 children are living with foster families. In 2010, 2,372 of the children living apart from their families were under the age of 5 years and 1,330 were 16 or older. 44.1% were white, 35.6% black, 9.2% Hispanic, and 4.1% American Indian.

Of the 4,467 children exiting out-of-home care in Wisconsin in 2010, 59.0% were reunited with their parents or other family members while 755 children were legally adopted through the public child welfare agency. Also in 2010, almost 30,000 Wisconsin grandparents had primary responsibility caring for their grandchildren. In the same year, almost 5,000 Wisconsin children were victims of abuse or neglect, a rate of 3.7 per 1,000 children. Of these children, 57.0% were neglected, 20.9% were physically abused, and 30.2% were sexually abused.

Children in foster care are vulnerable to maladjustment, given their exposure to both significant events leading to removal from their homes, followed by the exigencies of being in foster care. Despite the clear and compelling evidence that youth in foster care demonstrate both short and long-term, clinically significant mental health problems, the process or systems created that could meet their mental health needs are still rarely considered.

Chapter 14, Insight from an Adult Foster Care Survivor

Although I am 28 now, my experiences in foster care and adoption continue to shape me, for good and for bad. From my relationships with friends, family, and co-workers, to my religious beliefs and educational attainment, I would be hard pressed to think of an area of life that my foster care and adoption journey doesn´t affect.

I still remember how awful it was to be taken away from my birth mother without understanding why, and the horrendous abuse I and my younger brother suffered in the foster home where we stayed the longest. I also remember our adoption and how it felt to be reunited with my brother and to belong, for the first time, to a real family.

I remember seeing my parents at my college graduation where they showed up out of duty, followed by their divorce when I was in my early 20s, thinking how unfair it was to finally wind up with a family that really wasn't mine. I remember a call I received at 19 from a nurse telling me that my birth mother may die from cancer and then meeting my sister I hadn´t seen since we went into foster care.

While my feelings about foster care are ambivalent, my feelings about foster and adoptive kids still in the system are very strong. I don´t think any youth should have to go through the things my family went through without adequate community support, and I do not believe that support for those who are in or have left foster care is adequate.

Foster survivors go through tremendous emotional distress and upheaval as children, and we bear the scars from our youth into adulthood. Consider our vernacular or mismatched manners, or how we have to deal with PTSD in public and deal with depression we have to mask if we are to succeed.

Life is not easy, but adult foster survivors have to adopt chameleon like skills on top of dealing with gaps in education and common knowledge, in order to be hired for a job. If they can´t find a good job, they may not survive, much less prosper.

Mine was a hard job to land, but I am now lucky enough to work with foster teenagers. Each of "my kids" is facing the same struggle and fighting against the same odds as I did. We know without saying what loyalty is and how much we all care about one another and our families.

My teens have those deep, old eyes that tell stories of their own betrayals, rejections, hurt, and feelings of never being quite good or deserving enough. We share tales of how we, as former foster youth, can struggle so hard sometimes without anyone seeming to notice, and how we can still get hurt so easily.

* * *

I try not to convey this, but as you become older, you get even less help from the community. In fairness, though, learning how to be one's own support is a big part of becoming an adult. Therefore, I encourage my youth to find pride in their independence.

As when I was a child, I have moved often as an adult. It seems as if being a foster care survivor is to never be able to settle down, or not even knowing how to settle down. What creates stability? After fourteen years out of foster care, I can still only guess, but still haven't been able to incorporate stability into my life.

The way the world measures one, stability is a steady job, a steady relationship, a single place to live, and a strong community life. I hope that the teens I work with will be able to somehow achieve stability more effectively than I have. With the new programs out there, they probably will!

The *Jim Casey Youth Opportunities Initiative*, for which I am a site coordinator in the northern part of Lower Michigan, is one of two exciting ventures I can see making a positive change in foster kids' lives. Funded by *Casey Family Programs* and the *Annie E. Casey Foundation*, the initiative aims to help foster youth transition into adulthood without being so alone. Another good initiative, also funded by the *Annie E. Casey Foundation*, is *Family to Family*...a program helping foster youth remain in home communities and schools whenever possible.

I am excited about both programs because I think people are finally "getting it." **Keeping youth surrounded by communities,**

and having the community step in to help them, has more potential than anything else to help foster youth transition into successful adulthood.

I am often asked what made me successful, and I wish I knew! I'd love to be able to say that it was the youth I work with. While I was adopted at 14, I was basically left on my own when I turned 18. I haven't had a place to spend the holidays in a long time, and as an adult, I've still had to depend on my friends for the kind of help parents usually provide.

The years after my adoption were pivotal. Somewhere between 14 and 18, I went from hanging out at a crack house to college prep, and I will always be grateful to my adoptive parents for their help with that transformation. Many of my foster teenagers will never have that opportunity. I still think they can survive and survive well without it...if they can get enough love and support from their communities.

A lot of what my parents did was to show me a different way to live. I never wanted to be a failure, but was totally cognizant that everything in my life was leading me in a bad direction. Before my adoption, I had not even known there was a life of safety away from fears of rape, guns, or drug-addicted people. The environment my new parents introduced me to allowed me to finally grow.

But honestly, though I love them and am grateful, it's not fair to give my adopted parents all the credit. I've heard that it takes a village to raise a child, and I believe it. My strongest ability has been to make family members out of friends, and maybe ultimately that is truly why I've been successful; I've been able to make **my own support networks in the community**.

Hopefully I can pass that skill onto future generations of foster youth and maybe, as they learn how to advocate for themselves, their communities will embrace them. **Only a community of people can cure the loneliness, hurt, and fear in foster kids' hearts**, and only foster care alumni can appreciate how wonderful the world is for us when compassionate people reach out with the steadfast intention of making a difference. I owe a thousand thanks and much love to the many people who have made that difference in my life.

Chapter 15, Psychotropic drug abuse in Foster Care

In foster care as many as 2 out of 3 children are on psychotropic medications. In one sample of 300 children under the age of 7, 60% were on medication...in many cases reducing them to zombies. The culprits are Doctors pushing pills on 2, 3, 4, and 5 year old kids, at the behest of drug companies.

A major news organization spent a year studying this phenomenon nationwide by looking specifically at the states of Florida, Massachusetts, Michigan, Oregon and Texas where thousands of foster children were being prescribed psychiatric medications at doses higher than the maximum levels approved by the *Food and Drug Administration*. Hundreds of foster children received five or more psychiatric drugs at the same time despite absolutely no evidence to support the simultaneous use or safety of this number of psychiatric drugs taken together.

Out of nearly 100,000 foster children in the five states, more than a quarter were prescribed at least one psychiatric drug. They found that foster children were prescribed psychotropic drugs at rates up to nearly five times higher than non-foster children...with foster children in Texas being the most likely to receive the medications compared to foster children in the other four states.

According to the *General Accounting Office*, foster children in Texas were 53 times more likely than other children to be prescribed five or more psychiatric medications at the same time. In Massachusetts, they were 19 times more likely. In Michigan, the number was 15 times. It was 13 times in Oregon.

Foster children were also more than nine times more likely than non-foster children to be prescribed drugs for which there was no FDA-recommended dose for their age.

For the most vulnerable foster children, those less than 1 year old, foster children were nearly twice as likely to be prescribed a psychiatric drug compared to non-foster children. The shocking part was that babies under the age of one were receiving this kind of medication.

Dr. George Fouras, a child psychiatrist and co-chairman of the *Adoption and Foster Care Committee of the American Academy of Child and Adolescent Psychiatry* (AACAP), said that there was an incredible push to use medications to solve these problems as if it was a magic wand.

The stories include kids like 11-year-old Ke'onte from Texas, who testified before Congress about the overuse of psychiatric medications in foster children.

Neglected and often left home alone with his 1-year old sister, Ke'onte became a ward of the state at the tender age of four. Ke'onte was placed with a relative who, he said, beat him with belts, switches, and extension cords...which not only left him with physical scars on his body and understandably, with anger and despair.

The state of Texas bounced Ke'onte around six different foster homes and hospitals over a period of four years, during which his trauma was treated with an onslaught of psychotropic drugs...powerful mind-altering medicines such as the mood-stabilizer Depakote, the stimulant Vyvanse, the antidepressant Lexapro, clonidine for ADHD and the antipsychotic, Seroquel.

"I am not bipolar at all he explained" when interviewed on television. Nevertheless he was kept on as many as 12 psychiatric medications while in foster care...up to four of them at the same time.

"I was on a whole lot of medicines that I should not have been on"

He was one of the lucky ones out of every ten foster kids to be adopted by a loving family who made it their mission to get him off drugs and into therapy. His doctor has concluded that he doesn't suffer from ADHD and that he's not bipolar.

While almost all experts acknowledge that children in foster care have more emotional and behavioral issues, experts don't accept that this alone justifies the magnitude of the overuse of psychiatric medications dispensed to this vulnerable population.

Dr. Charles Zeanah, director of child and adolescent psychiatry at Tulane University says that "The general consensus is that when you're treating young children, you always try behavioral intervention before you go to medication."

Experts are also beginning to question the accuracy of diagnoses such as bipolar disorder and other mental illnesses in children, especially in foster children who may not always have access to comprehensive mental health services. The validity of these diagnoses is uncertain, and the fact of being in foster care may itself increase the likelihood of psychiatric conditions being diagnosed.

The *National Institute of Mental Health* reports schizophrenia affects just 1 % of the population and bipolar disorder less than 3%. And yet antipsychotics have become one of the top-selling classes of medications in the United States, with 2010 prescription sales of $16.2 billion.

Medicaid spends at least $6 billion per year, nearly 30% of its entire drug budget, on psychiatric drugs, more than double what was spent at the turn of the century.

Several factors may be contributing to the increasing number of psychotropic prescriptions for foster children:

Greater exposure to trauma before entering the foster care system;

Frequent changes in foster placements; and

Lax oversight by State authorities.

The *General Accounting Office* concluded that Texas, Massachusetts, Michigan, Oregon, and Florida each fell short of providing comprehensive oversight as defined by the *American Academy of Child and Adolescent Psychiatry* with regard to prescribing and overseeing the use of psychotropic drugs.

These states may not be following the oversight provisions required by law, according to the *Child and Family Services Improvement and Innovation Act* passed in September 2011 and the *Fostering Connections to Success and Increasing Adoptions Act of 2008*.

One state official told researchers at Tufts, that they needed guidelines to determine whether medications are needed and, if so, for how long.

Almost 50% of states either don't have, or are still in the process of developing, policies regarding foster care psychotropic drug use.

Antidepressants, anti-anxiety medications, antipsychotics, and mood stabilizers are some of the psychotropic drugs (psychiatric medicines that alter chemical levels in the brain, which impact mood and behavior). Of these antipsychotics, like Ke'onte's Seroquel and others like Abilify, Risperdal, Zyprexa, Geodon, Invega, Latuda, Fanapt, Clozaril, Saphris and Solian, are among the most powerful of these drugs.

Of all the psychiatric medications antipsychotics are, by far, the most prescribed, especially for foster children. They are given antipsychotics at a rate nine times higher than children not in foster care. While doctors aren't exactly sure how or even why antipsychotics work, most experts believe antipsychotics block specific receptors in the brain, which are thought to be overactive in patients with symptoms of psychoses, such as hallucinations and delusions.

Antipsychotics were initially designed for schizophrenia and bipolar disorder. Only Seroquel, Abilify, Risperdal, and Zyprexa have limited FDA-approval for use in children. Nonetheless antipsychotics are widely prescribed "off-label", meaning for conditions the FDA has not approved them for; such as agitation, anxiety, acting out, irritability, behavioral issues and even as sleeping aids.

Kids get aggressively diagnosed and sometimes we look for the easy solution, such as a pill rather than psychotherapy or simply better parenting.

Critics charge that, because of their sedating properties, antipsychotics are actually being used in foster care treatment facilities as chemical restraints.

They are trying to hide behind a nice shiny term that sounds as if they were just restraining a child when they were knocking the child out just to make it less of a problem.

This widespread and frequently unchecked use of antipsychotics is concerning, considering the serious side effects of these medications. Antipsychotics change a person's metabolism, frequently causing significant weight gain and an increase the risk of diabetes.

In addition to tremors, muscle spasms and restlessness, antipsychotics can cause tardive dyskinesia, a permanent and irreversible condition where a person has involuntary movements of the tongue, lip, mouth, and arms and legs.

Many experts are particularly concerned about the prolonged use of antipsychotics in children, given that there are absolutely no long-term safety studies for their use.

A recent Wall Street Journal article cautioned that children who were treated with antipsychotics had a threefold increase in risk of developing Type 2 diabetes as compared with similar children who were not taking psychiatric medicines. They advised to use the lowest dose for the shortest period of time."

Chapter 16, Children at Risk in Foster Care.

America has a nasty habit of stigmatizing the less fortunate. Children are our most vulnerable citizens struggling to learn what it means to grow up and be responsible. Those who enter this world in an abusive home have their chances of a decent life slashed by a society that forces them to live through needless trauma.

In a 2006 ABC News Report, Dr. Wade Horn, former child psychologist and *Director of the Department of Health and Human Services*, condemned the foster care system "as a giant mess that should be blown up."

He was most critical of the Federal Government's way of funding foster care with $5 billion aimed mostly at keeping kids in foster care. According to Dr. Wade, there were no provisions for treatment, prevention, family support or "aging out" at 18 years. The way things were set up was to keep everything exactly as they were, supporting the status quo. In his opinion the system needed fundamental change on a national scale.

His interview was an eye opener for many, although anyone taking a serious look at the foster care system would be in denial if not horrified that America's children were put at such risk and that many of their problems in adult life stemmed directly from their time in foster homes. The following is an exposé of the damage that can be done by the foster care system.

* * *

I was by no means a perfect child. I am not looking for sympathy or pity. I am a worthwhile person...warm, generous and intelligent. I have never been arrested. I have no interest in drugs, alcohol or dishonor of any type. I am one of the lucky ones who survived the foster care system by fighting hard not to give up.

My first few years of life were spent being hammered both physically by abuse and psychologically told how worthless I was. That, combined with the traumatic discharge from the foster care system, still has me believing at 25 years that I am not worthy of being loved with kindness. I had to find my self-worth on my own, because those charged with protecting and nurturing me, did almost nothing but inflict pain or low self-esteem upon me. Since then, my life has revolved around love, laughter, smiles...and hugs.

Unfortunately, the perils of the foster care system did not end with me, and it has now come back, like the ghost of Christmas past, to try again to make me a victim.

Throughout the 70s it was acceptable that the family pet had more legal protection than a child. I can remember watching a neighbor being taken to jail, eventually going to Federal prison, for kicking his dog across the yard. At the same time, my neighbors, teachers and the principal at my school could not get law enforcement to intervene on my behalf to stop the severe physical abuse which I suffered in my thirteen years of life. I finally forced the issue by running away with the threat to run again if they took me back.

Local law enforcement finally investigated while I sat in Juvenile Hall, finding more than sufficient evidence of the abuse I had lived through. They were actually amazed by what I had survived from 1975 until I aged out in 1980. Within those years, I was placed in more than 12 different facilities, including foster homes, a Baptist Home, another correctional institute, juvenile centers and group homes. I had to transfer to eight different schools.

My first foster home placement, at the age of 13, ended harshly when the son of a friend of my foster family sexually assaulted me. I appealed to my ultra-religious foster mother who accused me of lying and being promiscuous for which she removed me from her home.

She had pushed me into the church choir, Sunday school and other religious events, which I took on without hesitation and excelled in each. Yet religious views were the reason I was turned away. I have to wonder how many girls that boy assaulted after he got away with assaulting me.

I asked to leave my second foster home placement after two years, which was the longest placement I was in. I really loved my foster mom until another girl, who I had known to be dishonorable, joined the family. The bad karma between us severely stressed my mom and she wound up in psychiatric care. I asked my social worker to move me on the theory that it would help my mom recover. I was deeply wounded when she misinterpreted it to mean that I no longer loved her.

Twenty years later, when her husband was dying of cancer and asked to see me, she would still not allow me to come.

I was moved to a Baptist Home which may have had its heart in the right place but nothing else. One cannot trust "God" to protect the kids in dormitories full of bullies taking advantage of the kids with drugs, alcohol and cigarettes. There was more religion than there was security. Denial of a child's background and problems did not make any of it go away so the Baptist Home was no more than a temporary halfway house for troubled kids.

The subsequent correctional institution was a terrible experience. I would not wish it upon my worst enemies. It was an exercise in absolute conditioning. It reminded me of what this country did to Native American children when our government took them from their parents and tried to assimilate them by "teaching" the Native out of them.

One girl who I liked rather well had an attitude problem for which I could not slight her. She was gay and had been gang raped because of the fact that she was gay. Her parents really had a problem with her being gay but they refused to believe that she was raped and sent her to the institute for an attitude adjustment. It was expected that all the kids fit the "cookie cutter" mold of subservience, straight and totally obedient and if you did not comply, the correctional institute was the answer.

Kids were not allowed to have an opinion or to voice anything that did not fit their mold. We were expected to behave as Lemmings. I was the quiet kid and yet I ended up in solitary confinement twice in six months.

I ran away from the third foster home after being punished for not wanting to eat fried potatoes that were seasoned with a fried cockroach, and then told I was only in the home because they were being paid to have me...for that, I was given yet another label to stigmatize me. I was now "incorrigible."

I had been a quiet and docile sixteen year old kid up to that point. I did well in school, always called if I was going to be late, was respectful and considerate, was voluntarily involved with all forms of their religious functions...yet I was considered to be the problem child. This is the way for many children in foster care. If they are not problem kids when they go into the system, they become problem children because of the system.

The next trip to juvenile hall put me in the situation of either fighting or allowing an employee to get physically violent with me. I fought back to a degree but when it came to the right hook I threw at him, I swerved intentionally and hit the cinder block wall. I ended up in solitary confinement but it was better than going to jail for defending myself. That same employee ended up getting caught abusing another kid and eventually served jail time for child abuse.

More juvenile hall, foster homes and group homes came and went and then they turned me out without any support at age 18. I graduated from high school while in juvenile hall and I had to fight them to even allow that.

My father had died five years earlier and his social security checks, which were supposed to come to me, were being spent by the state. There were no more than three checks given to me in five and a half years.

* * *

When my children were born before the turn of the century, I became an easy target for anyone with a grudge, simply because I had been in the system as a child. In that state as a single mother at 20, I was "anonymously" reported for child neglect and was summoned to a meeting with a social worker to talk about the charge. I had walked eight miles and got to the meeting late.

I was forgiven and then informed of the charges. During the course of an investigation, the *State Social Services* had determined that the woman who had made the accusation coveted my daughter as her own to strengthen her marriage.

There was no basis for the charge but someone wanting to interfere out of her own selfishness had been allowed to put me on record for possible abuse...which had never occurred. This incident was the beginning of what would turn out to be the devastation of my family.

* * *

Since I had been in foster care, I was subject to abuse reports and it didn't matter how hard I tried to do the best possible job at parenting, an anonymous report could devastate both my child and me.

It didn't matter that I voluntarily took parenting classes, had no jail record, didn't do drugs or drinking, but I was still considered a "risk" parent because I had been abused. I was never told whether it was my mother's abuse or the abuse within the foster care system that was the reason that I was a bad risk, but I suppose it didn't matter. I sustained the physical abuse at home and the emotional and psychological abuse in the system that was charged with protecting me.

My only way out of this spiral was to get married, have another daughter, and move away to a distant state.

Chapter 17, Foster Care in England

Adapted from *"A Boy who lived at 35 Addresses"* as originally told by Ashley John-Baptiste in the BBC News Magazine:

I was placed in care at the age of two and remained in the system until adulthood.

I had four different homes during that time, three different foster families and spent several years in a children's home.

I've always felt being moved around so much, often very suddenly, without any real explanation, can really be damaging to anyone growing up. But I think actually I was one of the lucky ones, especially after meeting Scott, who in his early twenties was roughly the same age as me. He told me that he had been in care since he was six months old during which time he had lived at 35 different addresses.

"Some places were pretty good others were very bad. One set of foster care givers used to send me and my brother away for Christmas because they said that it was 'their' family time. So we never really felt like part of the household."

For many children in care the fear of being moved, especially if they have challenging behaviors, is a recurring nightmare.

"Often my foster parents weren't resilient enough. They responded with: 'this kid's a light weight. Let's move him out. There are thousands of other kids in care, we'll just get another one'" Scott explained.

It was one of many shocking things I learned on my journey of making a film for the BBC. Most horrifying was finding out that two of the boys I lived with in a children's home had been killed and a third was in prison having shot someone.

Having made this film, I've come to realize how different my life could have been and how much I owe my foster parents, who opened up their home to me, gave me stability and encouraged me to achieve a place at Cambridge University.

But even a successful foster mother, like mine, believes that a rethink is required on foster parents.

"It should be viewed as an important job. If they placed more emphasis on care givers, they'll encourage more good people to get involved.

"It's more than money, it's a vocation and if you're called to be a foster care giver, you do it wholeheartedly," she says with emphasis.

The outcomes for children growing up in care are not good. A third of the UK's homeless population stems from the care system and over a quarter of all prisoners grew up in foster care.

* * *

I met Jerome who grew up in care with his brother. After eight years in one foster home, Jerome and his brother were split up. Jerome remained in a stable home while his brother was shunted around the system. His brother is now in prison.

According to 22-year-old Jerome: "The more you move them, the more you scar them, because it's like you're just letting them know that people don't care about them."

"When you ask the kids what they want...they say simple things like, 'I want my foster care giver to give me a hug, or call me when I've had a good exam.

"They're the simple things. And none of it costs money."

Perhaps, most depressing is that half the people who grew up in care in England have children who are taken into care...which just perpetuates the cycle and to me it confirms that the start you get in life is all important. I truly believe that being moved around, as much as some children are, can cause long-term damage.

How can you be expected to move into adulthood as a productive member of society when you're so used to having the rug pulled out from under you? How can you complete your studies and do well in your exams if you're constantly on the move?

I met 18-year-old Sara, and helped her move from one hostel to another. She hadn't been given any notice, so all her possessions were in bin bags in the back of a taxi, surrounded by everything she owned. "This is as good as life gets for me." She professed.

I went back to see her in her new place a couple of weeks later and even though it was tiny, like living in a shoe box, she's settled in well and had even managed to improve her attendance at college.

I tell people that they can't change their past, but they can change their future.

"I don't want to be in the system no more. I don't want to be in the care system. I don't want to be in no benefits system," Sara responded.

She believes, like me, that education offers an escape route.

"If I have a good education, I can obviously get a good job."

Not everyone can be as strong as she is and who knows how she'll stay motivated if forced to move again? Sara's frequent moves are partly because of problems in the system.

The *Fostering Network* has described it as a "crisis" in fostering because of an overall shortage of investment in the system and other policy issues.

"The foster care system is bursting at the seams," Vicky Swain of the *Fostering Network* told me. Earlier this month, **the government announced the *Fostering for Adoption* plan** designed to streamline the process of placing children in care with their eventual adopters. It's a positive move and I welcome anything that gives children a sense of permanence and stability.

Once again I can't help but feel that all the emphasis from government and media is, as always, on adoption, to the detriment of the children who will never be adopted. They are always overlooked.

While we were making the film, I met a family that gave me hope.

Vicky had been fostered with her family for a couple of years. She wanted to stay with them and they wanted to keep her. They are not able to legally adopt her but during filming her local authority made her foster placement permanent, meaning that she doesn't have to worry about being moved again.

"You feel really lucky after a while and now there's nothing that I worry about," Vicky confided in me. "I'm the same as every other child, I'm just obviously not with my real mum and dad, and that's fine with me," she added.

The truth is that many of the 80,000 kids (in England) in care today will never be adopted...they're either too old when they enter care, or social services feel that there's a chance that their birth parents could one day sort out their issues and come back for them, regardless of how unlikely that really is. It's time that we put some emphasis and resources on them to make sure they're not left permanently scarred by never having a home or family they can rely on.

There were 65,520 children in local authority care in England during 2010, *about the same as the State of California*.

- 62% of them came to social services' attention due to abuse or neglect.
- 74% (48,530) were placed in foster care
- 3.8% (2,450) children were adopted as of 31 March 2010
- The average age at adoption was 3 years and 10 months.

Chapter 18, Aging Out Of Foster Care

It is hard turning 18...moving out, finding a job, going to college. But many foster children have to do it on their own, without a lifeline to parents and a home that helps most teens ease into independence.

Recent reports say that many former foster kids have a tough time out there on their own. When they age out of the system, they're more likely than their peers to end up in jail, homeless or pregnant. They're also less likely to have a job or go to college.

Life can be a struggle for these young people, even with help from the government and nonprofit agencies.

* * *

"We have an abrupt cutoff, like most states," Diane, who runs *Connected by 25*, a Tampa nonprofit agency trying to smooth the transition of former foster children, explained." You go from foster care, where you may handle $10 a month to suddenly being responsible for everything."

She says that things have come a long way in the last 10 years, when with their belongings in a plastic bag, foster kids turning 18, were taken to the nearest homeless shelter, since they had nowhere else to go, and left to their own devices.

"What we are doing is still not enough. It's like telling those aging out: 'Here's Option A: Fall off the cliff.'" she stresses for effect.

A new study...from *Chapin Hall*, a policy research center at the University of Chicago...finds that those who age out of foster care are not exactly falling off a cliff, but are desperately clinging to its edge.

An officer of *Partners for Our Children*, a policy center at the University of Washington, says that over the past eight years, he and colleagues from *Chapin Hall* have been following the progress of more than 600 former foster kids.

"Many of them are faring poorly. Less than half were employed at age 23 to 24. They're much less likely to have finished high school, less likely to be enrolled in college or have a college degree."

"In fact, by age 24, only 6% have two- or four-year degrees. More than two-thirds of the young women have children. Nearly 60% of the males have been convicted of a crime. Almost a quarter were homeless at some point after leaving foster care."

"Those children are our children, the children of society and of the state," Diane proclaims. "I would argue that we have no business taking them into care and then keeping them until they're in the transition to adulthood, unless we're going to try to do a good job of it."

* * *

Katrena, spent most of her life in foster care and still remained resilient. At age 24 her life had begun to stabilize. She has a job and a place for her and her 3-year-old son to live. It's a tiny duplex, but with a yard big enough for her to play with him when she comes home from work.

But it's been a long haul getting there. Katrena entered foster care as an infant and stayed until her 18th birthday. After aging out, she was OK for a while, but then she got pregnant, she stopped working and spent months moving from one friend's sofa to another.

"At that time I wasn't going to school, so it was hard."

Eventually, with the help of friends, some family members and the nonprofit agency *Connected by 25*, she began to turn her life around. Perhaps the biggest eye opener was having a child.

"It's just like suddenly you have another life that you brought into this world. And now everything you do, everything you own, everything you spend, is not yours, it's for your child now. So he's your number one priority," she emphasizes.

She still depends on food stamps, and on her landlord to cut her some slack when the rent is due. But she's back in school trying to earn her degree. She hopes someday to become a counselor for troubled youth.

* * *

Foster kids in group homes grow up in an alternative reality with too much structure, and too little love. They are unprepared and shocked to discover that the real world out there does not operate with the same uniform predictability that their group homes gave them.

The Chafee laws essentially doubled the federal funding allocated to kids aging out of foster care without families. It provided them with housing, training, and health care. Unfortunately the implementation was flawed. Nobody knew if the programs were working. One study sampled former foster kids in Illinois, Iowa, and Wisconsin. They were 24 years old by then. Half of them were unemployed and those who worked earned less than $8,000 per year, 40% had been homeless and only 5% of the men and 7% of the women had earned an associate degree.

They concluded that the system was giving these kids too little, too late. In reality the foster agencies just weren't good at it. It simply wasn't their mission. It gave caseworkers a carrot to offer their kids. If they signed themselves out, the laborious hunt for adoptive families would end. To an eighteen year old, three years sounds like a long time until abruptly it ends.

For eight years, researchers followed the 600 young adults out of the child welfare systems. At age 23 and 24, more than 75% of the young women had been pregnant since leaving foster care. About 60% of the young men had been convicted and over 80% had been detained.

Chapter 19, More on Aging out of Foster Care

Proponents of the existing foster care system don't like to be faced with the fact that, seen in totality, their foster care institution is hard at work creating our next generation of poor, homeless people. The U.S. Census Bureau estimates that 24,000 foster care children "age out" of care each year to find themselves without the skills to manage their lives. Less than half of them complete high school and the majority of them become homeless. Their rates of arrest, health problems, mental problems and welfare dependency are much higher than for children from ordinary families.

Foster youth is the only group involuntarily separated from their families through government intervention with the declared purpose of protecting them. However, at the end of the day, it is the government that will have to act as their parent to decide when they are ready to be out on their own. The "aging out" process inhibits that purpose. Turning 18 currently assumes that they'll be able to function in a way that non-foster kids are unable to do!

A typical youth placed in foster care at the age of 3, after living in 5 foster homes, is expected 15 years later to know how to care for him or her-self. The fact that there are many unhappy things associated with living in foster care that burden those "aging out" with perspectives not shared by ordinary 18 year olds, makes them highly vulnerable to failure and many of them sign themselves back in to age out at 21. To do so, they have to remain in school.

Independent living coordinators stress that foster youth can re-commit provided they were not perpetual problem children during care. More has to be done to let those who age out know that there are services available to them and that it is not just a case of someone standing at the door to force them out into an alien world.

The youth leaving foster care has already been burned by childhood experiences of abuse, neglect or abandonment in their birth families and subsequently in foster homes. Understandably, they are motivated to run away from the system, not thinking about, nor understanding the options that may be available to them.

All they have to do is sign a commitment that they are willing to pursue an education. In return the state will provide for them. However, there has to be effort on the part of the youth.

With child welfare in general and with foster care in particular, the problems that plaque these systems are community problems. Not county, state or Federal problems!

It's everyone's problem!

Youth aging out of foster care have to be made to believe that they have it within them to succeed and that they are qualified to do so. For them to believe that, in the overwhelming number of cases, requires a major overhaul of the existing foster care system.

As shown in a number of interviews in this book it only takes one person to make the youth leaving believe that there is someone in authority who believes in him or her.

There have been many changes to the system. One big change was *The Foster Care Independence Act of 1999* which aims to assist those aging out of foster care to obtain and maintain independent living skills. It recognizes that youth aging out of foster care, or transitioning out of the formal foster care system, are one of the most vulnerable and disadvantaged youth populations. At age 18, they are expected to immediately become self-sufficient, even though on average, according to the Affordable Health Care Act, children are not legally expected to reach self-sufficiency until the age of 26!

Many private and charitable providers of exiting services to foster youth, feel that the establishment already proved incapable to protect the youth during foster care and see no reason to trust them with post foster care services. The state workers on the other hand feel they are able to represent the youth in providing transition services. The question of why those same state workers, who were unable to draw better results from the failed overall foster program, would suddenly become capable of serving them during the transition to private life, remains obscure.

As in matters of education and environmental protection, we believe strongly that foster care should be made a community service as far as possible in which the national, state, county and township councils should play distant supervisory roles with a minimum of bureaucratic interference with community inspired care providers. Supervision should come from case workers operating independent of the foster home licensing authorities. The smaller the hands-on role of the Federal Government in the conduct of foster care, the better the experience of those in foster care will be.

Chapter 20, The State of the Art in Foster Care

Adults raised in foster care frequently praise their foster parents lavishly, because most foster parents do their best to give their kids a good upbringing. However, public policy has to account for parents who don't live up to such standards and to pay attention to what sociologists, psychologists and law enforcement say about the results in and after foster care.

The picture is not a pretty one. Much as we are trying to learn by interviewing youth recently out of foster care, one of many other studies interviewed children still in foster care and found that 70% of them blamed their caregivers for one or more of the following personal problems:

40% said their caregivers abused drugs or alcohol;

14% were found to be mentally ill;

18% had committed domestic violence;

10% had spent time in prison, and

34% believed their foster caregivers demonstrated inadequate parenting skills.

The results were that:

32% reported having been neglected;

13% reported child abuse;

2% reported sexual abuse by foster parents and;

17% claimed to have been sexually abused by a relative, a sibling or other foster kids.

In group homes sexual abuse is 28 times more likely than in overall population.

30% of the homeless in America and 25% of those in prison came out of foster care.

80% of children leaving foster care lead dysfunctional lives!

* * *

In California a recent audit revealed that more than 1,000 foster home addresses matched those of registered sex offenders. A Sacramento news source highlighted 600 of the offenders as high risk. The audit resulted from the death of a young boy in the foster care. Eight foster care licenses were suspended, and 36 orders were issued barring individuals from facilities.

Los Angeles County hired outside lawyers to resist exposing its results.

Independent child advocates say that it is common for girls to be raped and molested in foster homes. People involved in foster care are afraid to report widespread sexual abuse for fear of jeopardizing their federal funding.

The dominant national law firm bringing legal actions where abuse is prevalent, estimates that as many as 75% of all children in the foster care system, upon leaving the system, will have experienced sexual abuse. It is a heinous crime which continues to go unreported.

Disclosure of sexual abuse is often delayed until the injured child has become an adult. Research published by the *Canadian Centre for Child Protection*, concludes that only 30% of abused victims disclose it during their childhood.

They are vulnerable and typically have few social services available to them. A children's advocate in Saskatchewan concluded that foster parents begin by trusting the system when children are placed in their care to match the incoming child with the ones already residing in the home. Then belatedly they discover that the system doesn't care about appropriate matching and is focused on filling "available" beds. For private agencies, filling beds equates to greater profits.

To counter this tendency, critics of the system believe that the screening process for foster parents must be tightened and that case workers need closer supervision, preferably by an independent body. Certainly, the cases we present in this book militate in favor of that.

* * *

Study results inquiring into educational outcomes taken from the *Child and Adolescent Social Work Journal*, compared children in foster care with those living with at least one parent.

They found that foster kids dropped out of high school at much higher rates and were far less likely to complete their general education diploma. The ones who graduated received less financial assistance than those with parents or guardians. Foster kids reported more discipline problems in school and had to live with educational disruption from changing schools. They were less likely to be on a college preparatory high school track. Part of the problem is that foster kids are less likely to have care givers that monitor their homework. Of all the many disadvantages that foster children face, their low educational achievement has the most serious consequence in their future lives.

* * *

The young man interviewed for this book emanated from an overcrowded foster care system rife with problems which costs national taxpayers $2 billion a year. He wondered how anyone could justify spending so much to create the misery he experienced.

The experts say that 80% to 90% of foster care placements like his, stem from parental drug abuse. So what does society gain form spending all that money? Why not spend some of it on liberating the parents from their drug addictions?

A foster child is instinctively taught not to speak up. It's dangerous. And don't forget that mom or dad already gave up on you, so it's best to shut your mouth, or you could end up moving again. That was not our young man's style and he paid a heavy price for it. He believes that in the end it was worth all the agony, including beatings, with boards, paddles and razor straps which are common in group homes. He was beaten so badly at times that he thought he would pass out.

The grading system by levels, used in group houses is supposed to move inmates around to facilities with varying levels of security, depending on their behavior and psychological and emotional growth. We never saw signs of that happening in any group homes covered in the interviews we reported on!

In our young man's final group home, it became troublesome to adjust to different levels without some kind of defense mechanism. Since nobody gave a darn about him, he kept away from forming lasting relationships. Forming new relationships may now be one of his greatest challenges to be successful out here in the real world. He is struggling to find jobs while continuing his studies and it is nip and tuck whether he will realize his dream.

Former foster children have all seen jaded caseworkers who turn a blind eye, never ask probing questions and don't even visit their sleeping quarters during inspections.

To make things worse, there are statutes of limitation and other restrictions in place to limit prosecuting perpetrators or complicit state agency workers, after-the-fact. In this way we perpetuate massive corruption in our foster care systems.

If stability of family life is good for kids, foster care currently fails to do so. The average stay in foster care is five and a half years during which one will have stayed with an average of four and a half different foster families. That's roughly fourteen months per foster home.

About 37% of inmates will have run away from their foster homes and two-thirds of them will have done so more than once.

A spokesperson for the *Children's Defense Fund*, explained his shocking findings before a Congressional subcommittee. He said that children were physically abused, handcuffed, beaten, chained, and tied up, kept in cages, and drugged with psychotropic medication for institutional convenience!

A *Children's Rights Project* attorney testified as to the psychological death of many of these kids. She said that kids are being destroyed every day. Destroyed by a government-funded system set up to help them!

Each state must look hard at the outcomes it aims to achieve. Foster care people have to learn not to break a child's spirit just to make it more docile. The outspoken nature of some foster children is a sign of intelligence and confidence, and they will need those tools to make it through foster care emotionally intact. At some point in time, children may have to advocate for themselves because of incompetent professionals or abusive adults in their lives. One thing our young man could have used, as he tried to leave bad placements, was the big mouth he once had, before he was beaten into submission. On the other hand, our interview in New Jersey showed how determination and guts could beat the system and force complete liberation at age 16!

In Los Angeles County, 8 out of every 100 children are black. In foster care 29 of them are black. They say that when black children go into foster care, they get stuck there half as long again as children of other races. In his own experience our young man was discriminated against for <u>not</u> being black. He also found that the case workers he encountered were most frequently black.

There are over 18,500 children in foster care in LA County with more than 3,000 social workers to look after them. That's more than any system in America. There are tons of reports of shocking problems of child abuse, poor facilities, gross financial mismanagement and lack of supervision over the system. Instances of rape, sexual assault, beatings, forced medication and false imprisonment abound, and no one lifts a finger to do anything to fix it! (See Chapter 22)

* * *

A 2006 study reported in *Development and Psychopathology*, compared kids with similar at-risk demographic characteristics between those who:

- Experienced foster care;
- Were maltreated but remained at home; or
- Had experienced neither foster care nor maltreatment.

Psychological functioning affected foster kids most negatively.

Kids placed in out-of-home care exhibited many more behavior problems following release than kids who received adequate care.

Kids placed into unfamiliar foster care showed higher levels of internalizing problems than their pears outside of foster care.

All of this says that those who plumb for more and more kids to be taken from their parents and placed in foster care need to explain why those outcomes for children are preferable to what they might get at home.

Chapter 21, A Past Community Model.

My brother and I started life in a city south of Denver without our mother who had left us and when our loving dad died of tuberculosis, we were committed to a foster home on a farm with a large residence owned by an exceptional couple. Our new dad, besides farming, and our new mom besides being a nurse, gave us a marvelous frugal upbringing alongside their own three sons. After we "aged out" of foster care, they simply became our parents and we continued to live with them.

The woman responsible for child support services in our county and her lieutenant personally attended my graduation from college in the late ninety fifties, which left no doubt that they appreciated our adopted parents. So much so, that after we had grown up along with our three adopted brothers, they asked our parents to take on challenged high school teenage girls, all of whom had spent a good part of their lives in foster care.

Besides doing well at school each of the girls was expected to help with the many chores on the farm. In addition, our mother went to great lengths to give them music lessons during which she insisted on everyone learning to play the piano, before learning to play any other instrument.

She was superb in winning over even the toughest teen age girls through persuasion. She made it clear that this was their end of the line and that whatever they thought or connived to do, this is where they would stay until they were first class students. She would stay up all night with the most troubled girls if she had to, until they agreed to her first class dictions. She even had a full-length mirror in the hallway with inscriptions of how to examine them-selves before leaving on a first class date.

Out of well over forty girls only two failed the test and reluctantly had to be expelled.

She was very open with them to behave properly and held round table discussions in which sexuality was included.

At one point there was a death in the family in Kansas City which only our mom could handle and our dad had to step in and become more involved with the foster kids, since at times, there were as many as ten teen age school girls in the home.

Sundays were for going to church and each new girl was free to choose her denomination even if she had never set foot in a church. Attire for the occasion was most important so as not to ever let the side down. Some of the more musical ones would create choral presentations to perform at church functions. The emphasis remained firmly on being a first class act. As the foster mom put it, "some of the performers were so fussy they had more hang-ups than Zsa Zsa Gabor had in her wardrobe."

On top of all this, the welfare department came to see them to ask if they would consider giving house room to the children of a nurse in training until she became accredited. They lived with them until she could afford a home of their own. They often returned to visit her.

The big annual event was a huge Christmas Eve party to which all previous graduates of the foster home were invited. Their foster dad was the life and soul of the event and cleaned out the loft of the barn to put down fresh hay for the young offspring to sleep under his tutelage. It was a hilarious event with children of all racial and cultural backgrounds participating since these were the offspring of previous foster children. On one occasion a dark-skinned child asked him why she was so much darker than the other kids, in particular one of the very light skinned girls. He promptly explained that it was like toasting bread. "The blond kid was still not done, whereas she was." My 57 year old daughter, still talks about those Christmas events.

For a foster dad who worked in a saw mill and a foster mom who worked in a government office, their achievement in providing great foster care was truly remarkable. At his funeral service they had to block off half the space in the Chapel to accommodate his "children" and their offspring. His motto that one had to want to give back in order to live with one's conscience was vocally the theme at his interment.

The point of this story is that to be humane, foster care has to rely on the goodwill of communities. Unless it is maintained as a community service, as free from bureaucracy as possible, the system will remain prone to failure. **The consequence of such a failure is not socially sustainable and nationally the system has to change.**

Chapter 22, A Present Community Model.

I talked to a former inmate, now in charge of foster care operations at a non-profit, spiritually-based institution in which children in need of basic care can grow physically, emotionally, and spiritually. The goal is reunification of the families that come to them in need of support to grow confident young people with strong life skills. The facility embodies six cottages, a Community Enrichment Center, a Life Path house, a gymnasium, and a chapel caring for about 48 children who receive medical and dental care, counseling, and tutoring as needed in a warm and loving home under the care and guidance of well-qualified, full-time professionals.

Children from families unable or unwilling to participate under the right circumstance are taken into foster care in separate facilities consisting of a number of group and foster homes each capable of housing six foster kids and managed by a professional home mother or home father. A natural competitive spirit is encouraged between group and foster homes under their management in reconstructed homes acquired in the poorer districts of Dallas-Ft. Worth.

The gentleman we interviewed stayed on after aging out of foster care as an employee and grew into management positions until he became its executive manager.

Imbued with the dilemma of 18 year olds aging out without a protected living environment to move into, he started a supervised boarding house with training programs for inmates to gain the knowledge, skills and demeanor to become self-sufficient. In the course of learning, they take jobs to help defray their lodging expenses so that by the time they are ready to leave, they can make a living on their own.

So far the institution has served over 5,000 predominantly black children most of who moved on to become responsible citizens in society.

This is what we mean when we champion community involvement in foster care. We know of very few public bureaucracies in the United States and Canada that can come close to their level of performance.

We encountered upward of 90 such 501 (C) (3) institutions focused on the well-being of at-risk youth across America, some of them operating in multiple states with annual revenues in the billions. A particularly well qualified professionally-staffed operation on a ranch near Columbus, Ohio comes to mind.

In Los Angele's spectacularly dysfunctional system, tax exempt charities, specialized in the care of at-risk youth are the only bright spots in an otherwise dismal picture. **It takes a community to rise above child abuse!**

Chapter 23, LA Foster Care Spins out of Control.

According to area newspapers, Los Angeles County is suffering from an acute shortage of foster care beds and state officials are threatening to impose fines because too many children are too often languishing in chaotic holding rooms during traumatic separations from their families.

The problem intensified between May 28 and July 5, 2013 when nearly 600 children were diverted to holding rooms as social workers scrambled unsuccessfully to find homes for them with stays exceeding the 24 hour state limit.

Typically, children who get stuck in government-run way stations are the hardest to place. They are mostly infants, large groups of siblings, children returning from failed placements, the mentally ill and those afflicted with lice, ringworm, chickenpox, respiratory problems or other infectious diseases. Placing these children now requires more than a hundred calls by a social worker.

The county has to fix the problem quickly or face daily State financial penalties. A prominent law firm may bring legal action to force a resolution of the problems, in as much as the problem has been building for years.

Children below 12 get sent to the Children's Welcome Center on the campus of the Los Angeles County-USC Medical Center, to a large open space with cribs for infants and cots for other children, sleeping up to 29 children per night. They don't always have enough personnel to promptly feed children or change their diapers and send out emergency appeals for community volunteers.

Older children who can't be quickly placed in foster homes are typically sent to a conference room in a high-rise building south of downtown Los Angeles, where they sleep on the floor or on cots, sometimes surrounded by a mix of volatile teenagers, throwing objects and behaving so badly that police protection is required.

Hard-to-place children often run a bureaucratic gauntlet with social workers taking them to various regional offices across the county as the search for foster homes continues. If nothing is found, they are driven back to the holding rooms in the evening. During such placement hunts, they are not enrolled in school, have no rooms of their own and have virtually no privacy.

The county lacks an accurate, real-time, database of foster home vacancies. The system is updated once a month and only lists the licensed capacity of homes without indicating the number of beds the foster parents are willing to fill. Hence, social workers are left to their own contacts, experience and word of mouth to find vacancies. Offices with more experienced workers, as in the West San Fernando Valley, rarely use holding rooms whereas offices with newer social workers as in Hawthorne, Compton, South Los Angeles and Palmdale regularly have to resort to the use of holding rooms.

Over the past decade, the number of foster parents has declined faster than a reduction in children entering the foster system. The bed shortage is especially acute for infants, partly because the gap between the cost of caring for the children and what the state pays is the greatest for infants. California's reimbursement rate for very young children has to be increased by 61% to match foster parents' costs. The rate for children younger than 4 was recently boosted to about $680 a month. This is still hundreds of dollars short of the estimated costs of the foster parents. The rates are set by a remote state bureaucracy.

Los Angeles County is now entering into new contracts with private, nonprofit foster care agencies that are willing to accept children 24 hours a day.

Under threat from the State Government to take control, the County has decided to engage a czar with the power to clean up its decrepit, often corrupt, foster and group home licensing system.

Once again, community action trumps bureaucracy!

Edition Conclusion

Under-privileged youth in industrialized societies found themselves in urban communities as long ago as Charles Dickens. An era followed in which orphanages and schools for under-privileged children, was in vogue. The formation of child safety departments in local governments brought into being the concept of foster care in which, as a measure of last resort, licensed homes take in children as foster parents.

The state of affairs in foster care in industrialized societies is complex and in large part mirrors the morality of the least educated parts of their communities. It has become an integral part of displaced youth in urban environments.

The fact that child safety ordinances give their child safety personnel extraordinary powers to remove children from negligent parents and place them in licensed foster and group homes is at the root of serious problems. In any situation where private havens are licensed to receive and spend public funds, corruption in large urban settings is almost inevitable. The fact that foster children now only number 0.12% of overall population hides the reality of their plight. Even in such Counties as Los Angeles, foster kids still number less than 0.20% of host population and one seldom sees much written about their dreadful plight.

It does not have to be that way if the public will existed to change it. The money is being spent, but mostly wasted. In a modest way *The Foster Care Dilemma, Inc.* charitable foundation aims to enlighten the public without attacking well-meaning people now working within the system.

We expect to receive public input from many more people than the ones we interviewed for the publication so far, until future editions draw the attention of the New York Times best seller list.

About the Author

Born in the northeastern part of South Africa near the Lebombo Mountains, which form the border with Mozambique, **Johan Wassenaar** lived in a gold mining town in the Drakensberg Mountains called Pilgrims Rest where his father was the district surgeon. Below the mountains the game-filled Bushvelt stretched as far as the eye could see. That is the country which always lived in his soul. He came to North America as a young engineer with expertise in thermodynamics and went to work in the aviation industry in Canada during the Cold War, the object being to outpace the Soviet Union in defense capability. He became wrapped up in secret schemes to frustrate them. this work led him to Los Angeles, then the creative center of America.

It all ended with the war in Vietnam, which historically may be seen as America's nemeses. He formed an international strategic planning consulting business to help large high technology companies adjust to changing conditions while also acting as marketing VP to revitalize a diversified industrial manufacturing corporation. Later on he helped found a motion picture company in Santa Monica and moved his family to Hope Ranch in Santa Barbara. He later became interested in horses in Santa Ynez Valley with an extra-vocational interest in managing competitive dressage shows. His interest in energy conservation systems continues as does his work on green energy projects. In 2002 he began writing and publishing novels, which now include the following:

Love in the Shadows of Apartheid a trilogy comprising **Teresa**, **Sharon** and **Inge**.

The thriller, **Die for me Argentina** and the **Sex & Love Trilogy**, featuring **Sadism**, **Love** and **Consequences**.

The Foster Care Dilemma is his new non-fictional series of books.

www.ingramcontent.com/pod-product-compliance
Lightning Source LLC
Chambersburg PA
CBHW071224280526
45787CB00002B/801